WILLA CATHER
The Woman and Her Works

WILLA CATHER

The Woman and Her Works

MARION MARSH BROWN and RUTH CRONE

Charles Scribner's Sons   New York

To the memory of our parents, ever young in heart

MMB
RC

A-8.70 [c]

Printed in the United States of America
Library of Congress Catalog Card Number 76-123838

FOREWORD

After Willa Cather's death, Keith Ingersoll, Grand Manan teacher, historian, and curator, wrote Edith Lewis, the novelist's long-time friend, regarding Willa Cather's date of birth. In one reference, it had been stated that it was 1873; in another, 1876. Miss Lewis answered: "Yes, the date of Miss Cather's birth was given as 1876 in *Who's Who*; but E. K. Brown's researches seem to have established it as 1873. It never occurred to me to ask her when she was born!" (This discrepancy had previously been discovered and published by James Shively in his *Writings from Willa Cather's Campus Years.*)

The date on the tombstone at Jaffrey, New Hampshire, is 1873, but one may well wonder whether or not this is particularly important, for her literature represents far more than her own life span.

Her writings extended, too, beyond the boundaries of their settings, though these have significance. Each of the co-authors of this book, native Nebraskans, at early ages became imbued with Miss Cather's works. With undergraduate study, this interest increased until it became an adult absorption. Having collaborated on one book, the authors embarked on this. Setting again played a role in that, in the process of their research, the authors traveled to various places where Miss Cather had lived, interviewing many who had known her—acquaintances, tradespeople, friends, relatives, colleagues, neighbors, critics.

MMB
RC

5

ACKNOWLEDGEMENTS

Surely no one can write a book by himself. Nor can two persons write a book by themselves.

The authors of this book are no exception.

To the others who helped in many ways to make this volume what it is, we wish to express our grateful appreciation.

First among these are the people who kindly gave us insights into Miss Cather's life and character through sharing with us reminiscences of their friendship or association with her. Of great help also were those who directed us to such persons.

Particularly helpful on the Red Cloud years of Miss Cather's life were Mrs. Carrie Miner Sherwood, Mrs. Mildred Bennett, and Miss Josephine Frisbie.

Material from the Pittsburgh years was generously supplied by Mrs. George Seibel and Mrs. Anna Lindsey, and by former high-school students of Miss Cather: Mrs. William Lindsey, Mrs. John Dale, Mrs. Herbert S. Brewer, and Mr. C. H. Klingensmith.

Of especial help in Jaffrey, N. H., were Mr. and Mrs. Ed Brummers, Mrs. George Austermann, Mrs. James Bowers, Miss Virginia Hunt, Mrs. William Royce, and Mrs. Warren Ruffle.

Among the most helpful on the Island of Grand Manan, New Brunswick, were Miss Dora McLaughlin, Mr. and Mrs. Ralph Beal, Mrs. James Buckley, the Misses Ethel Manning, Katharine Schwartz, Eloise Derby, Sabra Jane Briggs, and the Messers. Herbert Macaulay and Keith Ingersoll.

To Mr. Yehudi Menuhin and Mr. Stephen Tennant go

our especial thanks for their kindness in sharing sensitive insights into Miss Cather's later years.

Through correspondence with several other persons, we felt we came to know Miss Cather better. Especially responsive were Mrs. Rachel Condon Takes and Mrs. Anne L. Young and Mrs. Viola Hays, former students of hers; Cornelia Otis Skinner (Mrs. Alden S. Blodgett), whose parents had known Miss Cather; Mr. and Mrs. Charles Savage, proprietors of an inn at Northeast Harbor, Me., where the writer visited; Richard E. Truesdell, a former bellhop at Shattack Inn in Jaffrey; and Mr. and Mrs. S. Phillip Colehour, whose detailed responses were among our joys.

Too, we had kind letters and interesting conversations, coast-to-coast, with many others: Mrs. Gordon Anderson, Homer Belletete, Professors George K. Anderson and Edward Bloom of Brown University, Commodore George Boudey, Clyde Robert Bulla, Mrs. Clarence Bucy, Mrs. Lawrence A. Cather, Homer Dilettuso, Mrs. Joseph L. Fournier, Mrs. Sadie Harshman, Catharine Hunter, Mrs. E. J. Lampson; Marcella Powers; Mrs. J. P. Scott; Margaret Strauss; and W. L. White.

Librarians and historians were oftentimes among our best friends. Other than those previously mentioned, these include: Janet M. Agnew, Bryn Mawr College; Mrs. Horace Chapman, St. Peter (Minn.) Subscription Library; Donald Dankers, Nebraska Historical Society; Mrs. James W. Saxon, Washington & Jefferson College; and Mrs. Josie P. Stone, Nicolett County (Minn.) Historical Society.

Certain newspapers and various of their personnel were particularly cooperative. The *Jaffrey Ledger* came to our aid; the *Boston Traveler* was helpful; and staffers of the *Pittsburgh Press* did service above the call of an advertising fee.

We are pleased, too, to mention grants received from the Municipal University of Omaha (now, The University of Nebraska at Omaha) and the State of Wisconsin for assistance in our research. For the former, awarded to Mrs. Brown, thanks go to then-President Milo Bail, Dean Robert

D. Harper, and English Department Chairman Ralph Wardle; for the latter, awarded to Miss Crone, to administration and colleagues at Superior State College (now, The State University of Wisconsin at Superior).

Our sources were not always domestic; one of the foreign scholars of American literature whom we highly regard is Mrs. Fumi Takano, Professor of English, Tsuda College, Tokyo.

Background material was appreciatively discovered in Mary Watkins Cushing's *The Rainbow Bridge* (G. P. Putnam's Sons, N. Y., 1954); in Burton Rascoe's articles; in a pamphlet by Alfred A. Knopf ("Publishing, Then and Now, 1912–1964," the twenty-first of the R. R. Bowker Memorial Lectures, N. Y. Public Library, 1964); in E. K. Brown's "Homage to Willa Cather" (*Yale Review,* V. XXXVI, No. 1, Sept., 1946); and in James Weber Linn and Houghton Wells Taylor's *A Foreword to Fiction* (D. Appleton-Century Co., Inc., N. Y.-London, 1935.)

In other areas we had assistance also. Keith Krecklow, Gage County (Nebr.) Soil Conservationist, gave us a brief but to-the-point course regarding "The Divide."

Three who read portions of rough draft and made thoughtful comment and criticism included Mrs. Richard Dustin, Mrs. Francis Geer, and Mrs. C. A. Anderson. Other of our friends took a personal interest in helping with various facets of the research, including Ethel Pehrson, Mrs. John Webster, and Mr. and Mrs. Robert Peterson of St. Peter, Minn.; Pearl Shockley and Marion B. Andrews of New York; and James and Ellen Shively of Mankato State College, Mankato, Minn.

To all those who showed patience and understanding and who gave us encouragement we are appreciative.

MMB
RC

CHAPTER I

In the peaceful, snow-clad hills of Frederick County, Virginia, on December 7, 1873, the turbulent spirit of Willa Cather was born. Charles Cather, her father, was a sensitive young man, as handsome in appearance and quiet in nature as the Back Creek countryside. Her mother, the former Mary Virginia Boak, was an attractive young woman, whose sparkling vitality presented a striking contrast both to her environment and to her husband's personality. Their union made for a happy, fun-loving family.

At the time of their marriage, the young Cathers had gone to live with Mary Virginia's widowed mother, in the home in which Mary Virginia had grown up, and it was here that Willa was born. Mrs. Boak was a practical, efficient woman, who had raised her children alone following the death of her husband, an honest, aggressive, and effective politician.

Not far from the Boak home lived the elder Cathers, in a big, square, brick house, Willowshade. The land on which it stood—three hundred acres—William Cather, with determination and hard work, had acquired piecemeal over the years. This paternal grandfather of Willa's was admired in the community for his strength and tenacity; though something of a religious and political rebel, he was highly respected. His wife, who had been Emily Anne Caroline Smith, was a Back Creek native, healthy, industrious, and an estimable homemaker. She was, in her way, as strong a character as her husband.

The ancestral strains of sensitivity, industry, vitality, and tenacity were to become fibers in the Willa Cather pattern.

While the inherited warp would always remain, the environmental woof was soon to change. The year after Willa's birth, her Grandfather Cather had paid a long visit to his son George, who had homesteaded in Nebraska. From that time on, William Cather had talked of moving his farming operations from the difficult, rocky hills of Virginia to the level plains of the Midwest.

When Willa was three years old, her grandfather made his decision, and the elder Cathers left Willowshade for a farm they had obtained in Webster County, Nebraska. So Willa, with her father and mother and Grandma Boak, moved into the big brick house at Willowshade.

This was a wonderful house for a little girl to explore, and Willa let no opportunities go unexploited. Too, there was the joy of being carried on her father's shoulder to see the new lambs or to watch the dogs drive the sheep from a clean-cropped pasture to a verdant one. Indoors or out, there was always activity to interest a small girl: the churning of butter, the baking of bread, the piecing of quilts, the shearing of sheep, the mowing of hay, the picking of apples.

And there were people coming and going: hired help, relatives come to visit, itinerant peddlers and preachers. There were plenty of bedrooms for the aunts and uncles and cousins; and even the itinerants were often "bedded down" in the one-story ell at the back of the house.

As time went on, there was one baby brother to add to the excitement at Willowshade, then another, and a baby sister: Roscoe, Douglass, and Jessica.

While the other children were still too small for Willa to play with, she spent much of her time with the hired girl, Margie Anderson. Margie was somewhat retarded mentally, but she was good company. She told Willa stories, many of them true, of the men and women in the Valley, and she had a flair for the dramatic which made her tales memorable. Margie was also interested in the things around her, and when she and Willa took walks in the woods, they made discoveries which were exciting and satisfying to both: the first violet in spring, the bright speckled fish in the creek, the perfect blood-red maple leaf in fall.

For several years Willa knew the serenity, the security, the peace, and the joy of this good life in Virginia. Then, when she was nine, she was catapulted into a change so violent that it was like being thrown into a stream of cold water. Her father and mother had decided to join Grandmother and Grandfather Cather and Uncle George in Nebraska.

"Nebraska" meant little to Willa when the family began talking about the move. More real were things that must be left behind. The house and its familiar and loved nooks and crannies. The farm and the sheep and the milk cows. The woods and the creek. The people—neighbors and friends and relatives. Fortunately, those who were nearest to her outside her immediate family were going too, Grandma Boak and Margie Anderson.

Yet the wrench was severe, and as the pens were emptied of their livestock and the house stripped of its furniture, the little girl who had felt at one with it all was deeply shaken.

But soon there were the exciting train ride and startling new scenes to turn her thoughts. Nebraska was still a very young part of the country. Only sixteen years before, the state had been admitted to the Union. The early settlements in the territory, made prior to the Civil War, had been largely along the Missouri River on the eastern border. Settlement along the Republican River in the section to which the Cathers migrated had not begun until 1870, a scant thirteen years before the arrival of Charles Cather and his family.

What a change from Virginia with an order already nearly as well established as that of the Old World!

However, once settlement had begun in south-central Nebraska, it had grown rapidly, for the land was fertile and the terrain made it easy to cultivate. The combination of "the good land" and its availability for homesteading had enticed numerous ethnic groups.

The settlement of Red Cloud was fourteen miles southeast of the farm on which the Cathers were to make their new home. Here they arrived by rail on a raw spring day. Totally unlike the comfortable countenance of the Virginia villages, the unbelievably stark face of a frontier town greeted them.

It had no mountains, no hills, no woods—not even trees to give privacy or shade. There were no brick houses—only little white boxes spotting the faint green landscape. Grandfather Cather, though, pointed out with pride the brick opera house and the brick bank, standing tall on Main Street. What a scenic shock to a small girl!

Then came the trip by carriage for the adults, by "spring wagon" for the children and baggage, out across the prairie to "The Divide," the watershed from which the water drains southward into the Republican River and north into the Little Blue. And now the contrast with Virginia was even greater—breathtaking, startling; for there seemed to be no end to distance. Gone was the feeling of a small world, intimate, embraced by the everlasting, tree-shrouded hills. In its place was vastness, unbroken vistas whichever way one turned, coming to an end only when the curve of the earth met the sky.

In addition to the impact of the new land, the impact of place, there was the impact of its people. A few miles away from Cather land in every direction were excitingly different men, women, and children; it was to these that Willa was drawn as she rode horseback over the countryside, discovering and exploring. Some she found living in "soddies" built from blocks of native prairie sod, crowded little dwellings which were warm in winter and cool in summer—secure against the elements but not against slithering snakes that dropped from the rafters. The people living here had come but recently from the Old Country, bringing with them their native dress and speech and habits of living and thought.

However, not all of the people Willa discovered, as she

rode the countryside, lived in the luxury of sod houses. Some, where the land was rougher, lived in "dugouts," caves in the sides of hills.

In one settlement she found Bohemians, in another Germans, in another Swedes, in another Danes, in still another French Canadians. Of them all, the Bohemian families drew her most strongly. They were people who, with determination and hope, were fighting for survival. People with great fortitude and endurance. Like a many-antennaed bug, with all antenna at alert, the young Willa observed and absorbed, feeling deeply their predicament. As later revealed in her stories, the characters and their setting were inextricably meshed.

The months she lived on the farm were months of freedom close to the absolute. She did not attend school. Her Grandmother Boak had taught her to read and write while they were still in Virginia, and she continued to teach her now; yet lessons were not a set, patterned part of her life. Nor were household tasks arduous. Even though she was the eldest child in a fast-growing family, there were Grandmother Boak and Margie Anderson to help with the housework.

This life on the Divide, however, was to be brief, for after a year and a half of farming, Charles Cather decided that he was better suited to life in town than on a Nebraska farm. So in the fall of 1884, he sold his cattle and farm machinery and moved his family to the town of Red Cloud, where he opened a land office. The days of complete freedom for Willa were gone.

CHAPTER II

Willa's activities in Red Cloud, though more confined, became more intense than when the Cathers had lived in the country. In town, the family was crowded into a rented story-and-a-half house, with the children's sleeping quarters in the "half"—an unfinished attic. Far from feeling put upon, Willa was delighted with this sanctuary away from adults. The raw rafters were much more curious than plastered walls. There were even chinks through which one could squint at the stars, and through which snow sifted in winter. When Willa became older, she developed a haven all her own in one small room of the attic, covering its walls herself with rosebud-patterned paper, and arranging a few hand-me-down furnishings—a bed, a washstand, a chair, a desk—to complete her nest.

Meanwhile, her first friends in town were neighbors, the Miners, who owned and operated a prosperous general store. Willa tagged after the Miners' eldest daughter, Carrie, four years older chronologically. Yet Carrie was to say, "She was a grown-up with me; always she was an adult." Willa's favorite times for talking seriously with her friend were mornings when Carrie was combing her hair and preparing to go to work in her father's store.

"She would sit at the end of my dressing table . . ." said Carrie.

About what did they talk?

"Everything. Willie was interested in everything—events and people"—from Carrie's young men and the dances and socials to which they took her, to the town feud involving allegedly mishandled county funds. What people were like and why—from the Miners' Bohemian hired girl, Annie Pavelka, and her family, to wealthy former Governor Silas Garber and his beautiful young wife. The stories and the "What-do-you-thinks?" and the discussions went on endlessly.

"Well, what then?" Willa would say the minute the conversation showed the slightest tendency to falter. Carrie's father would ask, "Don't you ever get tired of that child's questions?" To him, "that child" was a pest.

The younger Miner children found that their new playmate's imagination led them to high adventures. They built a town of packing cases carried laboriously from Miners' store to the Cathers' back yard. Here, along the fence in the plum thicket at the south side of the house, they ranged their buildings. Some of them were two stories high—packing box stacked upon packing box. So grew "Main Street" until it contained a millinery store, a candy store, a post office, a hotel, a city hall, and a newspaper office. They named their town "Sandy Point" for the sand pile nearby, and elected Willa its mayor. Grandma Boak, on baking days, served hot bread to the citizens of Sandy Point.

Then there were the expeditions to the island in the Republican River, which beckoned Willa's brothers and their friends as well as the girls, for here were to be found all kinds of adventure, from real fishing to pretend hunts for treasure.

And there were trips to the railroad depot, a mile across town. When a train was coming in, excitement ran high. Down the train steps to the brick platform might come a sprightly dandy, a shuffling salesman, a family of weary settlers, or a glamorous theatrical troupe. The baggage car might disgorge, along with slouchy mail sacks and mysterious boxes, a wooden house of the dead.

Of the travelers, the occasional theatrical troupes provided the most immediate stimulation. The children presented plays which Willa often wrote, or adapted from something she had read, and which she always directed.

17

There was the one about a doctor, his wife and his patients, with Willa in the leading role. Mrs. Miner helped Willa fit one of her brother's old suits for her costume, and the play was presented in the Miner home. There were double doors opening from the parlor into the dining room, an arrangement ideal for the children's theatricals. With the doors closed, the cast dressed and prepared their stage in the dining room. When the young actors were ready to begin, the doors were opened and the guests, ranged in chairs in the parlor, were ready for the performance. This drama was called "Dr. Alle," and played to a full house: the Miners, Cathers, Weiners, Hollands, Garbers, and McKeebys—the last named being the Cathers' family doctor and his wife.

The amateur theatricals were such a success that, after the Blizzard of '88, the children decided to put on a play to raise funds for the people who had been impoverished by the storm. This time they enlisted adult aid, secured the Opera House for their performance, and presented "The Beauty and the Beast." The forty dollars earned went to buy groceries for those who were most in need.

When Willa was eleven, she took part in the Sunday-school program at the Baptist Church. Bow and arrow in hand, she recited "Hiawatha" with great eloquence, and, true to the lines, "Then, upon one knee uprising, Hiawatha aimed an arrow," she took the proper stance and shot into the "forest," which her audience could almost believe was there.

Those who disapproved of young Willa thought she carried her histrionic talents offstage. They were particularly convinced that she affected a pose during a period when her ambition was to become a doctor. She had her hair cut as short as a boy's. Then, apparently enjoying the mild sensation made by her haircut, she donned clothes belonging to her brothers, to parade about the town.

The three M.D.'s in town, however, dissected Willa's behavior as she herself dissected the bodies of cats and frogs, and found, under the bobbed hair and the unfeminine attire, an intelligent, questing mind intent upon discovery. Dr. McKeeby respected and had an affection for the girl, eager to learn, willing to help, and often took her with him as he rode the countryside in his buggy, making his rounds. Dr. Dammerell also took her on calls with him; and Dr. Cook, who owned the town drugstore, allowed her to help him in the store, paying her with books and other items from his stock.

Willa had other adult friends. The Weiners, who lived next door, were among the first, and any "stages" Willa might go through would not shake their friendship. The Weiners were a Jewish couple, who spoke both French and German fluently, and whose home bespoke cultural richness through the paintings on the walls, the books lining library shelves, and the sophisticated conversation which took place in it. Mrs. Weiner welcomed Willa's visits, gave her free access to the library, read French classics to her, translating as she read, and opened her house to the girl as a second home.

Another adult friend was Willa's music teacher, Professor Schindelmeisser, an elderly German itinerant who had drifted into Red Cloud and settled down for a time to give piano lessons. At first, Willa as a pupil was a source of frustration to him, for it soon became evident that she cared nothing about learning to play the piano. All she wanted from her teacher was to hear him play and talk about great musicians, about European cities, about anything that would give her vicarious experience of a world beyond her own. This, Schindelmeisser did not consider the prime function of a music teacher.

However, upon confiding in her mother that his pupil was not learning piano and suggesting that she give up her lessons, he discovered that Mrs. Cather felt it was worthwhile for "Daughter" to learn the things he could teach her *about* music. From then on, the relationship between teacher and pupil changed, and the old professor reveled in his young pupil.

William, or "Uncle Billy," Ducker, another village store-keeper, whose true love was more literary than commercial, also became a staunch friend and strict mentor to Willa. He was teaching his own daughters Greek and Latin, and added Willa to his list of students. He gave freely of his time to read the Latin poets and the Greek philosophers with her, not only teaching their languages and literature, but also discussing the civilizations they represented.

Another friend was Mrs. Peorianna Bogardus Sill, named for her birthplace, Peoria, Illinois. She had studied both art and music abroad for fifteen years and was sympathetic to Willa's interests in the arts and in things European. Willa was impressed as she watched Mrs. Sill conducting an oper-etta or a cantata, dressed in a floor-length velvet gown and wearing diamond earrings purportedly given her as a wed-ding gift by Washington Irving, a distant relative.

The Red Cloud high-school teachers to whom Willa par-ticularly appealed were Mrs. Eva J. Case, who taught liter-ature and foreign languages, and Mr. and Mrs. A. K. Goudy, who were superintendent and principal, respec-tively. Mrs. Case encouraged Willa to get out of the small-town environment of Red Cloud to where there were greater possibilities culturally and fewer restrictions on being oneself.

One of the most significant of Willa's friendships with adults was that with "the First Family" of the community, former Governor Silas Garber and his wife and son. Silas Garber had been a captain in the Union Army. Sometime shortly after the end of the War between the States, he had heard stories of the Republican River Valley with its oceans of tall red grass and land to be had for the asking. With his two brothers, he had come West in 1870 and chosen the site that was to become the town of Red Cloud. To file on land under the Homestead Law, he had to ride horseback 120 miles to Beatrice, Nebraska, location of the nearest Home-stead Office.

Silas Garber plotted the town; he represented his part of

the state in the Nebraska Legislature; and in 1875, he was elected governor. At that time, he was a widower with one son. During the early part of his term in office, he went to California to visit his brother; there he met and married the sister of his brother's wife, a charming young Southern woman, vivacious, lovely to look at, and considerably younger than he.

By the time the Charles Cathers moved to Red Cloud, the Garbers had a fine home on the outskirts of town. They entertained frequently and handsomely; their guests were important, influential people in government and industry. Willa was also entertained by them, informally, on many Sunday evenings, most often in summer when picnics in the Garbers' five-acre cottonwood grove were in order. And she went for drives with Mrs. Garber behind her beautiful, high-stepping little mare.

Then there were those who were more earthy, not of the "intellectual class," but from whom Willa learned much. There were, for instance, the Lambrechts, a German family who lived in a dugout on the Divide, where Willa visited them frequently. Mrs. Lambrecht welcomed her into the kitchen, showed her how to prepare favorite German dishes, answered this inquisitive child's questions with pleasure. After the Cathers moved to town, Mrs. Lambrecht brought them fresh farm produce almost every week.

In this group also was Mrs. Newhouse, who owned the house Charles Cather rented for his family. She, too, was German born. She had no use for snobbery or "the elite," was both outspoken in her praise of the new land to which she had come and open in her derision of those who did not have the stamina of the first-generation pioneers.

Despite the understanding of these friends, Willa knew she was being criticized in some quarters—particularly because of her vivisections. She defended herself in her commencement address when, with two boys, she was graduated from the Red Cloud High School, June 5, 1890. She entitled her address "Superstition versus Investigation," and her thesis was that it is the sacred right of man to investigate and that all progress depends upon scientific investigation. In developing it, she did not hesitate to refer directly to critics of "inexperienced persons" who called these novices "cruel." "Nevertheless, if we bar our novices from advancement, whence shall come our experts?" she asked.

One must pursue the truth.

CHAPTER III

Willa's parents believed that truth was founded on knowledge and that knowledge was to be gained through formal education. Their eldest child, the only one of their three girls whom they called "Daughter," would therefore be given the opportunity to continue her education. Charles Cather had read law in Washington, D.C., for a time; he was of a scholarly turn of mind and would be proud to finance her at the University of Nebraska in Lincoln.

But Willa's schooling, though culminating in a high-school diploma, had been most erratic, and the Admissions Office at the University considered her inadequately prepared to enter its college classes. They placed her in their Preparatory School in September of 1890.

One of her classmates later recalled Willa's first appearance in class. Having had difficulty finding the room in which the group was to meet, she made her entrance after the door had been closed and the class had begun, so all eyes turned toward her. She closed the door and strode to a seat, not at all disconcerted by her tardy entrance, opened her notebook, and turned her attention to the professor.

She wore a skirt that showed a couple of inches of her ankles. This in itself was scandalous! In addition, her coat was of distinctly mannish cut. With it, she wore a plain white, starched shirtwaist with no ruffles, embroidéry, or frills, and—most amazing of all—a flat-brimmed, round sailor hat atop a head of bobbed hair. This in 1890! This in Lincoln, Nebraska!

As the days and the weeks of the preparatory year went by, Willa leaned heavily toward studies in the humanities rather than in science. Her fellows and professors saw in her a young woman with a good mind, though not the most brilliant in her class, rather opinionated and prone to argue, but pleasant and interesting.

At times, some of her instructors thought her annoying, for if she were not interested in a subject or a particular lecture, she made no attempt to conceal her lack of zeal; rather, she made it blatantly obvious. A case in point was related by her seatmate in an English class. There were double seats in the classroom, and Willa and this young woman had taken a back seat at the beginning of the term. Rather than listening to the professor, they preferred to entertain each other. Willa wrote verse to divert her seatmate; the seatmate responded by drawing pictures to entertain Willa. Both verses and drawings were extremely amusing to the two girls and resulted in much giggling. The professor, finding this distracting, soon moved the girls to a seat immediately in front of his own desk.

Here it was difficult for the young ladies to continue their pleasant pastime, so Willa, never at a loss for ideas, turned to arguing with the professor. One argument she deliberately carried on so long that he forgot to ask for the themes due that day. Willa had been unprepared to turn in a theme, but far from unprepared to meet the emergency. Her strategy had been successful.

Later, in the University proper, Willa engaged in vociferous disagreement with Dr. Lucius A. Sherman, Chairman of the English Department, regarding his analytical method in the study of literature. He disliked this, but liked her writing.

Though other of her English teachers found her irritating at times, they also found her stimulating, for she was well read, had ideas, and was able and eager to express them. Her mathematics teachers, on the other hand, found her inattentive. She was not interested in mathematics, did not understand it, did not like it, and did not do well in it. In fact, she failed to make a satisfactory grade in a required course during her freshman year and received "a condition," which would be removed if she passed an examination after further study. She did not attempt the examination until her senior year, and in the interim, was considerably concerned about the possibility of failing it and, therefore, not being graduated. In later years she admitted to a recurring bad dream in which she saw herself sitting outside the professor's office, waiting for his decision as he read her make-up exam. In her dream, when the door opened and the professor emerged, it was to announce that she had failed the examination.

However, in reality she did pass the make-up test and was given credit in the course. In the meantime, she often held forth in strident tones, to all who would listen, about how the University was not going to keep her from graduation just because it required her to take mathematics, which she abhorred and found a complete waste of time.

There were those on the fringe of these harangues who smiled at her boasts, though "the inner circle" nodded approval or clucked their sympathy, for Willa had her admirers, even as a freshman.

It was during her freshman year that she acquired the nickname "Billy," and even though her hair was permitted to grow the following year, the nickname remained. It was also during that year that she said good-bye to science. She took only a beginning chemistry course. Then something happened which turned her ambitions in another direction than medicine.

Professor Hunt, while reading a set of themes in fulfillment of an English assignment for which Willa *had* been prepared, came across one which excited him. It was on Carlyle, and it was written by Willa Cather. He was pleased and impressed at the ideas it expressed, the critical sense it exhibited, and the flow of words. As he went on to read the others, the typically pedestrian papers, the contrast between them and Willa's made him resolve to see if his friend Charles Gere, editor of the *Lincoln State Journal,* would

25

publish the Cather paper. Mr. Gere readily agreed to run it.

When the essay was published, it was accompanied by a brief Editor's Note, which caused nearly as much comment as the publication of the essay. "The article," it stated, "is original work from the literary department of the University of Nebraska. The writer is a young girl sixteen years of age who comes from Webster County. A careful reading will convince any student of literature that it is a remarkable production, reflecting not a little credit upon the author and the university."

Mr. Gere, without having met "the young girl from Webster County" had formed a high opinion of her. His daughter Mariel was attending the University, so Willa Cather was invited to the Gere home. There was also another Gere daughter, Frances, and both of them, as well as their mother and father, became friends of Freshman "Billy" Cather.

Mrs. Gere, when someone commented that she didn't see why Willa wanted to be so "mannish," said with a smile, "She doesn't want to." Mrs. Gere's persuasion, capped by the offer of a coveted role in a Greek play, was responsible for Sophomore Willa's letting her hair grow.

Her circle of friends in Lincoln also was growing, though it was to remain comparatively small, select, and of her own choosing. Besides the Geres, there were the Westermanns, a large family of means and culture, with sons in the University; and the Canfields, the "head" of which family was also the "head" of the University, Chancellor James H. Canfield, whose daughter Dorothy was later to make a literary name of her own.

While many of her contemporaries on campus admired "Billy" Cather, few were drawn closely to her. As several of them were to say, "We respected her, but we did not love her."

During those first years in college, Willa spent much of her time studying conscientiously in the solitary confines of her bleak quarters in a rooming house. She had to keep her own fire burning in a small, pot-bellied black stove, carrying scuttles of coal up two flights of stairs. Her classmates felt that she did not care to waste time in frivolities or idle chatter. Yet they did not think of her as "a loner." She joined the Union Literary Society; the other members enjoyed her contributions in dramatic roles and elocution. But their association with her remained casual. The young men were put off by the weighty discussions upon which she embarked and the vehemence of her opinions; the young women could not talk clothes or beaus with her. Yet they were proud of having her in their organization.

In her sophomore year, Willa began working on school publications and was pleased that she could get things done. She was literary editor of the *Hesperian,* a small magazine published bi-weekly; the following year she became managing editor. A young man, B. C. Mathews, who wrote editorials for the magazine, recounted that she had "positive ideas," but was not overly critical or dictatorial about his work.

There was another young man, however, who had a very different opinion of her.

Besides the *Hesperian,* there was, on the Nebraska campus, a monthly paper originally called *The Lasso,* but later, *The Nebraskan.* To it Willa contributed a regular column, entitled "Pastels in Prose." A fellow student, E. C. Ames, thoroughly disapproved of the column and its author. In his opinion, she was far too critical of everything and everybody; he considered her prejudiced and unjust, at times even cruel. Seething, he read her columns for several months and then decided to write a column himself, in which he would "take Billy Cather apart." This he did, submitting the piece under the title, "Postals in Paste." Then he sat back to see what would happen and, very soon, to gloat; for not only was his column published, but "Pastels in Prose" ceased to appear.

Years later, he was still venomous about "Billy" Cather and could see little that was praiseworthy in her writing. As far as he knew, he said, she had no friends at the University of Nebraska and wanted none.

This was, of course, not strictly true. Mariel Gere became a close enough friend to visit Willa at her home in Red Cloud during summer vacation. Dorothy Canfield, considerably younger than Willa, admired her writing and was grateful when Willa collaborated with her on a story published in *The Sombrero*, senior yearbook of 1894.

During Willa's junior and senior years, through her association with the Gere Family, she began publishing some columns in the *Lincoln State Journal*. Now townspeople also came to have strong opinions about her.

There was quite a coterie of Lincoln families who considered themselves and each other well-educated, cultured, and refined. They supported and enjoyed the traveling stock companies which brought drama to the city.

So, when "a young upstart of a University student" wrote a column in anticipation of Julia Marlowe's appearance in a forthcoming Sheridan Knowles' comedy, they pursed their lips. In part, Willa wrote: "Heretofore a great actor has seldom dared play anything but Shakespeare in Lincoln . . . . The great uneducated public have a sort of idea that Mr. Shakespeare was a great playwright, and as he is the only playwright they know anything about, they admire him very much."

And what she wrote of Sarah Bernhardt, after a Lincoln appearance of the famous and beloved actress, shocked them: "Bernhardt's really great acting is limited to the expression of just one passion . . . . All [others] are . . . clever imitations; only one is genuine with her . . . . No other actress has ever lived who could love on the stage like Bernhardt. It is so genuine that . . . it seemed wicked to look at her. . . ."

To Catholics, the jibe, "We have a St. Patrick's Day in memory of nonsense," was sacrilege; to friends of J. Sterling Morton, exponent of planting and preserving trees, Willa Cather's remark that "Arbor Day [is] in memory of nothing whatsoever" was a flippancy; to all and sundry good church people, her phrase, "a Thanksgiving day in memory of blessings we never get" was blasphemy; and to all who held the Constitution in esteem, the phrase "a Fourth of July in memory of a document that is largely a dead letter" was little less than treasonous.

Yet there were those who considered some of her judgments to have merit and contemplated thoughtfully such statements from her column as: "After all, art is soul, perhaps it is the only thing which gives art a right to be."

Another local newspaper, *The Courier*, in an editorial comment about Lincoln journalism, said, ". . . on the whole, the dramatic criticism is something to be proud of. Toby Rex of the *News* and Willa Cather of the *Journal* have done capital work, and their writing is admired and enjoyed by intelligent and discriminating people."

The editor of *The Courier*, after Willa Cather's graduation from the University in 1895, offered her a position with that newspaper. An item then appeared saying, "Miss Cather's reputation extends beyond Nebraska. She is thoroughly original and always entertaining. Her writing has a piquant literary flavor, and her services are a valuable acquisition to any paper."

But her remaining time in Lincoln and in Nebraska was to be brief. Very soon, she was to go out from the state of her young years, though she would not go out of the lives of the people who had known her.

CHAPTER IV

In June of 1896, one year after her graduation from the University, Willa left the Midwest for the East. On a visit to the Geres' in Lincoln, she had met their houseguests, Mr. and Mrs. Charles Axtell and daughter from Pittsburgh.

Although the Axtells thought Willa somewhat Bohemian, Mr. Axtell was impressed by her ability as a journalist. He was in the process of launching a small Presbyterian magazine, *The Home Monthly;* after his plans had matured, he had written Willa, offering her the job as editor.

Willa had been living at home, though still doing some writing for the Lincoln papers. And while her family had been patient, they had been eager for her to show some tangible results of her ability and of her college education. So she was elated about leaving, sarcastic and mocking concerning Nebraska, though time was to prove the state had been good to her. Still lacking this perspective, however, she conceived of going to the East as a release and an adventure.

When Willa arrived in Pittsburgh, the Axtells took her into their home until she could find suitable living quarters, but, significantly, they had bundled their daughter off to visit relatives.

Also, fearing unorthodoxy, Mr. Axtell laid down hard and fast rules for his young editor. He recognized her ability, but thought he also recognized a waywardness of thought which would not be in keeping with the kind of magazine he and his associates proposed: a simple, wholesome, "fireside" journal; entertaining, and above all, "pure."

He soon relaxed, however, for Willa was obeying orders. She had her own reasons for doing so. This job meant her freedom. It was the channel for her escape from "the plebeian Midwest." In it lay the seed of her opportunity to "show them" back home.

She soon found lodging in a boardinghouse close enough to the office of *The Home Monthly* so that she could ride to and from work on her bicycle. Each weekday morning, racing the streetcars, she pedaled so furiously that the spokes of her wheels became glinting discs.

Her co-workers on the magazine saw little of this frolicsome side of their editor's nature. To them she presented much the same image that she had to her fellow workers on the University of Nebraska student publications: a young woman extremely well organized, with amazing vitality and devotion to hard work, who could not only get a job done herself, but who likewise could see that others got theirs done.

They discovered, too, soon after her arrival, that a shortage of copy for a given issue of the magazine caused her little concern: She could always dive into her own stockpile of manuscripts and come up with something to fill a gaping space, or could quickly dash off a few lines for a filler.

Inevitably, the areas in which Willa began to make friends in Pittsburgh were in the arts. For Pittsburgh, though it presented an ugly, coal-sooted, and depressing façade to most, revealed to the starry-eyed young Willa Cather a strong, red-blooded cultural heart. The wealth derived from coal and iron, oil and gas, was evidenced not only in the city's mighty steel mills and belching factories but also in concert halls and theaters, in art museums and libraries. Andrew Carnegie had only recently endowed the cultural center to be known as The Carnegie Institute; it had opened its doors to the public the same year Willa Cather came to Pittsburgh. She lost little time in finding her way to it.

May Willard, its librarian, began to take an interest in

the young woman who checked out armloads of books at a time. It did not take her long to discover that this Willa Cather who signed her name on the library card with such a flourish was an editor.

Soon the casual relationship of librarian and patron developed into friendship. From May Willard's friendship it was but a step to that of Edwin Hatfield Anderson, chief librarian at Carnegie.

Another librarian Willa met was George Seibel, who became a contributor to *The Home Monthly,* and invited its editor to his home. The Seibels lived all the way across the city from where Willa resided, but having once taken the long streetcar ride to their home, she was never again to consider the distance far. The Seibels made her one of the family; after Baby Erna had been put to bed, and supper and the dishes were behind them, George and Helen Seibel and Willa Cather read and discussed French Literature with enthusiasm and delight. One of Mr. Seibel's favorite authors was Flaubert, and he happily discovered that Willa had a similar penchant.

For her part, Willa was appreciative of having made friends with a family, for, living in cheap boardinghouses, she found little of the warmth of home. She and the Seibels became lifelong friends. Helen Seibel was to say after the death of her husband and of Willa, "Our friendship lasted as long as she [Willa] lived . . . . We loved Willa Cather, and she was a wonderful friend all her life."

Mrs. Seibel did not take it unkindly when Willa told her that she was tired of seeing little Erna always dressed in white, as the criticism was accompanied with a gift of lovely soft pink cashmere. After Helen Seibel had made the material into a beautiful dress, she admitted the color was much more becoming to the child than white.

In the concert hall of the Carnegie Institute, Willa heard the celebrated musicians of the day (Victor Herbert conducted the symphony there.) and in its gallery saw paintings both old and new.

She also frequented the theater. In the Pittsburgh stock company, Lizzie Hudson Collier was the much-admired and loved leading lady. Willa soon joined her devotees, and with the excuse of a column she still sent back to the *Lincoln Journal*, she met Mrs. Collier. The actress warmed to her interest, and a friendship developed. At times, Mrs. Collier treated Willa almost like a daughter.

On one occasion when Willa appeared at the star's dressing-room door, she refused to step over the threshold, explaining in a hoarse whisper that she had "a terrible cold" and wouldn't want to risk giving it to Mrs. Collier. The actress scolded her for being out when she should have been home in bed, and exacted from her a promise to come back to the dressing room after the final curtain. Upon returning, Willa found to her amazement that Mrs. Collier had a cab waiting to take the two of them to the Schenley Hotel where the actress was staying. "I am going to take you home with me and put you to bed," she said, and over Willa's protestations, she did just that, mothering and nursing the girl until she was well enough to be up and about again.

At the end of its first year, *The Home Monthly* changed hands, and Willa considered this a good time to resign from a publication whose basic tenets failed to arouse her enthusiasm. She obtained a job with the *Pittsburgh Leader,* a daily newspaper with the largest circulation of any evening paper in Pennsylvania.

With this change came more money—seventy-five dollars a month—and with it, too, a decided change in daily routine and duties. At the *Leader,* Willa had the telegraph desk, and most of her time was spent in editing and rewriting the news that came in over the wires. This was not particularly stimulating, once the novelty had worn off; but two advantages developed from the new position: First, her desk was next to that of the music critic, Mr. Burgoyne, and through him she made numerous contacts with personalities in the musical world. Second, in a short time she was allowed to write dramatic criticism for the paper.

Mr. Burgoyne found the new telegraph editor a joy; he liked her frankness, tenacity, and integrity. She was intellectually stimulating. And, with her deep blue, very alive eyes and her mop of chestnut hair, she was attractive though not a beauty. He was proud to introduce her to the friends and acquaintances he had made in music circles.

One of the friends, Mrs. John Slack, frequently invited Willa to the musical soirées she gave in her home in the fashionable suburb of Sewickley. It was here that Willa met Ethelbert Nevin and his wife, next-door neighbors of Mrs. Slack, and the young editor was thereafter a guest in their home on a number of occasions.

Except for the area of opera, with its drama, Willa did not venture to express criticism in the field of music. While she enjoyed music greatly and attended nearly as many musical as theatrical performances, she realized that the meagerness of her background, knowledge, and understanding rendered her incompetent to judge.

Once during Willa's early days with *The Leader,* Dorothy Canfield, who also enjoyed the arts, came to visit. Willa took her to the Seibels' to help trim their Christmas tree, a special occasion that year because it was little Erna's first Christmas.

Dorothy Canfield was impressed. She liked the Seibels. She thought it "quaint" that Willa and George Seibel were plotting how they could buy a complete set of Stevenson's works which they had seen in a bookstore. Even between them, they did not have the price of the set they coveted; so Willa volunteered to see if the proprietor of the store would let them have the books if they made a down payment on them and promised to pay the remainder at so much a week. This was an innovation in 1897, daring and practically unheard of. Yet the agreement was made, and the Stevenson books went home to the Seibels.

During the latter part of her four-year stay with the *Leader,* Willa snatched time from her job to do some writing other than newspaper copy. In her last year there, no columns or articles appeared under her byline. Instead of using the time outside office hours to write additional newspaper copy, she was using it to write copy for a literary magazine called *The Library*. In the twenty-six issues of the magazine which were published, there were twenty-four pieces by Willa Cather. They ranged from poetry to short stories to factual prose.

And the editor of *The Library* was not the only one responding favorably to Cather submissions. The same year saw poetry by Willa Cather published in *McClure's Magazine, The Critic,* and *The Criterion,* important national magazines. Furthermore, one piece of fiction appeared in the *Cosmopolitan,* and an article in *Ladies' Home Journal.*

Willa Cather was in her late twenties. She had been out of the University for six years; she had been in Pittsburgh for five. She had served an apprenticeship. At last prominent editors were beginning to take notice of her, and she wanted more time to write.

CHAPTER V

She wanted and needed more time to write. But one must earn a living.

After some thought and consultation with friends, Willa decided to try for a teaching position. Then, hopefully, her hours on the job would be fewer; and she would have her summer vacations free for writing.

She was hired for a position in Central High School in Pittsburgh, a college-preparatory school, to teach English and Latin. This was the fall of 1901. She was several years removed from her own study of Latin, and Helen Seibel recalled her saying that "she had to brush up on her Latin over the weekends in order to keep ahead of her class." Still, the teaching position did allow more time for writing than had her job with the *Leader*.

One of Willa's students, Anne Lindsey, said, "She had to depend on inadequate trolley cars [for transportation], walk several blocks up a steep grade, then climb four flights of stairs to freshman classrooms on the top floor of the building, but was still keen and forceful enough to make the instruction interesting."

Miss Cather maintained a sufficient degree of aloofness to keep her class well in control, but was nevertheless friendly. She had a sincere interest in her students and a good sense of humor. Most of her pupils thought she wasn't a bad sort as teachers go.

Sometime during this year, in Mrs. Collier's dressing room, Willa met a contemporary, Isabelle McClung, member of an old, stable, cultured family. Her father, Samuel A. McClung, was a judge. Isabelle's home and way of life were affluent, but her upbringing had been strict, and against this and the society in which she lived, she was in some rebellion. Her interests were in the arts, and although she herself had no particular talent, her taste was excellent and sure. Her enthusiasms were for reading, the theater, and music rather than for afternoon teas, drives in the park, and the parties at which her friends spent their leisure.

When she met Willa Cather, she was immediately interested, for she had read her dramatic criticism in the *Leader* as well as some of her poems and short stories in various periodicals. People who were producing in some field of the arts were the people whom Isabelle McClung admired and enjoyed. Not only was Willa an author, but also her interests paralleled Isabelle's. So the dilettante pursued the acquaintanceship, which grew rapidly into friendship.

Having discovered that Willa was living in a drab boardinghouse, and thinking of the space in the McClung mansion, Isabelle invited her to become a part of the McClung household. There has been some disagreement as to the way Willa was received in this family. Her biographer, E. K. Brown, has indicated that Isabelle McClung succeeded in securing her friend a place with the McClung family by threatening to leave home if she did not get her way in the matter. However, according to Edith Lewis, Willa's longtime friend, "she [Isabelle] apparently had no difficulty in persuading her father and mother to invite Willa Cather to become a member of the McClung household." And Helen Seibel said, "If Willa Cather had thought the McClung family opposed to her living with them, nothing would have made her do it as she had too much pride to stay where she was not wanted." However the decision was made, Mrs. McClung welcomed Willa immediately; the Judge was slower to respond, but did come to respect and enjoy her.

She was given a room at the back of the house. It had previously been a sewing room. There she had the peace and quiet she needed to do serious writing. And at last she was in the kind of environment in which she had always felt she belonged! It was something like being at the Weiners' in Red Cloud: There were books and music and fine art pieces and intellectual conversation. But in addition, there were ease and elegance here, which she had not known in any previous situation. With well-trained servants, with solid and extensive financial resources, with a secure place in Pittsburgh society, the members of the McClung family lived what seemed to Willa an ideal life—and now she was a part of it.

She finished the year at Central High School; then she and Isabelle went abroad for the summer. In this experience also Willa found splendid fuel for creative fires.

To help pay for her trip, she contributed to the *Lincoln State Journal* a running column of commentary on her travels. These columns reflected the impressions made upon her by her first contact with European cultures. They were chiefly of four kinds: historical or traditional, literary, human, and sensory. And while the pupils in her classes the following fall felt more of the impact of the first and second, critics reading her books in later years were to see a greater reflection of the latter two. For her style was to be rich with sensory images; and her sensitiveness to people and their problems, a dominant feature of her books.

Disembarking at Liverpool, England, the two young ladies traveled first to Chester. In the column Willa wrote there, she remarked on the ruins of the walls of the ancient city, then moved on to the history of the Old Castle and its splendid Norman tower. "My friend and I," she wrote, "spent half of a June day in almost utter solitude at the foot of the tower. . . . The temptation to attempt to reconstruct the period when these things were a part of the living fabric of the world is one that must necessarily assail an ardent imagination."

The same feeling was evoked for her in France, at Avignon: "How to write of Avignon, the fine old city of the popes . . . its history alone would make it one of the most interesting towns in France."

The impact of the past touched Willa Cather through her ability to imagine the long-gone time and the people who then lived.

With her love of literature, she of course made literary pilgrimages, with Isabelle her willing companion. They traveled to Shropshire, near the Welsh border, to see the country which produced A. E. Housman, whose poetry Willa greatly admired, and later—with Dorothy Canfield who had joined them—to make an unannounced call upon the poet. To Rouen in France, the home of Gustave Flaubert. "One of the first things that greets your eye in Rouen is the beautiful monument erected to Flaubert in the very wall of the Museum. . . . Just across the walk . . . is his friend and pupil Guy de Maupassant." To the old French cemeteries: Montmartre and Père-Lachaise, to find the graves of Alexandre Dumas, Heinrich Heine, Alfred de Musset, Honoré de Balzac.

But Willa's interest in the people she saw, and the sights and the sounds and the smells that assailed her senses found their way constantly into her columns and showed that they were the things which were of prime importance to her.

From the fascinating "Canal People," living in boats at Chester, the London shop girls, the Italian immigrants, and the "gin-soaked . . . working-folk" of London's East End, to the French peasants harvesting their wheat, she showed her intense interest in the common man.

Of the laborers in the fields at Barbizon, she said: "After the rakers and stackers came the gleaners—usually women who looked old and battered, who were bent and slow and not good for much else. Such brave old faces as most of these field-working women have, such blithe songs they hum, and such good-humored remarks they bawl at a girl who sees too much of one particular reaper. There is something worth thinking about in these brown, merry old women." Perhaps they reminded her of the immigrants on the Nebraska farms among whom she had grown up. Perhaps they all merged into one impression, which she was to use later with great power in her portrayals of character.

After Dorothy had left them, Willa and Isabelle crossed the Channel to France. When Willa first saw French soil, it was in the early light of dawn. As usual, her senses were alive, discriminating, tuned to receive the finest nuances in sight, smell, taste, feeling. "The black water broke in long-lashed, regular waves toward the shore," she wrote. "The sky was black behind us and grey before. . . . The high chalk cliffs of Normandy were a pale purple in the dim light." The little fishing village of Le Lavandou she saw as "all green pines and blue sea and a sky of porcelain. . . .

"It is good for one's soul," she wrote, "to sit all the day through . . . and do nothing for hours together but stare at this great water that seems to trail its delft-blue mantle across the world." She mentioned the scent of dried lavender always in the air and the touch of the pine needles "dropping on one."

Finally, with the time to return to home and duties drawing near, the two friends came back to Provence and found the smell of autumn in the air. "The country of tambourines and Muscat wine. . . . It is a high, windy, dusty country. . . . The vineyards are red as October oak leaves," Willa said in her column. "The smell of . . . making wine is everywhere. . . . The sycamore leaves are beginning to turn a little, . . . and in the evening there falls the chill of autumn, the strange, homesick chill. . . ." These final impressions went deep.

And so the journey ended, and Willa, filled with the "good wine" of her summer sojourn, returned to Pittsburgh and teaching.

For the school year of 1902-1903, her salary was increased from $650 to $750—almost 20 per cent—evidence of the appreciation of her work. And during that year, her first book was published. It was a small volume of verse,

April Twilights, and although she had now been in the East nearly seven years, the "twilights" were Nebraska ones.

When she had received her few author's complimentary copies, she journeyed with one to the home of her friends, the Seibels, and presented it to George Seibel. On the flyleaf, she had written, "To George Seibel, the first and kindest critic of these verses."

It was 1903 when this volume appeared, a dozen years after the publication of the first editions of Emily Dickinson's poems. Yet the Cather poems showed none of the originality of form, none of the forecast of the "New Poets" of the twentieth century which characterized Miss Dickinson's. Willa's were formalized, rather artificial, and imitative. They revealed the influence of the classics, of Rossetti, and of Housman.

Yet the little poem, "Prairie Dawn," showed promise:

A crimson fire that vanquishes the stars;
A pungent odor from the dusty sage;
A sudden stirring of the huddled herds;
A breaking of the distant table-lands
Through purple mists ascending, and the flare
Of water-ditches silver in the light;
A swift, bright lance hurled low across the world;
A sudden sickness for the hills of home.

And there was something in the poems or in her short stories which were appearing in magazines, or in both, that caught the eye of Publisher S. S. McClure. He would watch her. Willa Cather was gaining stature, not only among her pupils, co-workers, and friends, but among editors and the literati.

In the fall of 1903, Willa did not return to Central High School, but she did continue teaching for three more years —at Allegheny High School in a suburb on the north side of Pittsburgh. Her predecessor in the position was a friend, Preston Farrar, who resigned to do graduate study, and his influence and that of an uncle of Isabelle McClung's helped Willa to make the change. The distance from the McClung residence to Allegheny was considerable, requiring early rising of the young teacher who spent many late evenings at the opera, at concerts, and at the theater. Yet she did her job well and also did some serious writing during those years. Her pupils, as at Central, generally accepted her as a "good" teacher, though some disagreed. And the editors of some of the best magazines: *McClure's, Scribner's,* and *Lippincott's* accepted her stories.

With the close of her third year at Allegheny, came an end to the decade Willa spent in smoky but cultivated Pittsburgh. In 1905, two of her short stories, "Paul's Case" and "A Sculptor's Funeral," had been published in *McClure's Magazine.* Then S. S. McClure brought out her first collection of short stories, under the title *The Troll Garden.* The book created no furor. The influence of Henry James, whom Willa greatly admired, was strong in these stories. Yet they showed some originality. The last in the collection, "Paul's Case," was one of the best. The use of her experience as a high-school teacher for setting, environment, and understanding of the adolescent character, gave this story reality and freshness.

Sam McClure, sharp as a fragment of shrapnel, read the signs correctly. He came to Pittsburgh and offered Willa an editorial position on his magazine. She accepted.

Though it was getting a rather slow start, for Willa was already in her thirties, the talent of which only small, immature samples had as yet appeared, was soon to be unleashed.

CHAPTER VI

The year was 1906. *McClure's Magazine,* founded thirteen years before by an immigrant Irishman, S. S. McClure, was a magnificent chapter in a Horatio Alger success story. In the comparatively few years since its inception, the magazine had attained a stature unprecedented in American publishing. In fact, it may well have been "the best general magazine ever to be published anywhere," as Peter Lyon, Sam McClure's biographer, said. It was the first general magazine to sell for fifteen cents a copy, when others were selling at twenty-five and thirty-five cents. It was the first magazine in the United States to pick up the big political and economic issues of the day and treat them fully and factually in well-written prose. It was the first to run a series of personality sketches on famous people, and the first to secure all the top names for its fiction list.

But by the time its editor-publisher contacted Willa Cather in regard to joining his staff, the magazine and its tempestuous founder had had a number of ups and downs, and at the moment, he was "down."

Sam McClure had met Willa Cather in 1905. He liked to meet his authors face to face and talk to them—doing most of the talking himself. So it was that he had breezed in at the McClung home in Pittsburgh unannounced, stayed to dinner, talked brilliantly and continuously, and breezed out. But before he left, he had invited Willa to visit him and his family in New York.

When summer vacation had freed her from the classroom, she accepted his invitation. She spent a week with Sam and Hattie McClure and their children. There was immediate, mutual respect between Sam McClure and Willa Cather, each admiring both the talent and the strong life-force of the other.

But in the late winter and early spring of 1906, Sam McClure was in trouble. He had built up an organization with some of the strongest editorial material in the country. However, with his fantastic imagination and daring hand, he himself controlled all, and his associates had begun to question his judgment and demand a change. They finally insisted that he either sell out to them or buy them out. He bought them out and they left.

Nearing his fiftieth birthday, Sam McClure must start over. He wasted no time. He would build another staff as fine as that which had deserted him. One whom he summoned was Willa Cather.

When the school year was out, she answered the summons. She moved to New York, which was to be her home for the rest of her life, and was made an associate editor of the magazine. Most of the others assigned to important positions on the staff were also new. The atmosphere of the editorial offices, with Dynamo McClure hurling his ideas at his personnel, then leaving them to meditate, was exciting and stimulating.

During off hours, Willa, with the help of a friend, found a place to live in Greenwich Village. It was in sharp contrast to the luxurious home on Pittsburgh's Murray Hill. She took a studio apartment on the south side of Washington Square, in a building old and musty, but filled with other aspiring artists like herself. Most of these Bohemians were younger than she; Willa was now thirty-three. They observed her at a distance, walking in the square or striding off to work each morning, keeping regular hours in contrast to their highly irregular ones; and they did not consider her a true Villager. Willa, on her part, observed both her Greenwich Village "compatriots" and, with especially keen interest, the children and old women of the Italian population living nearby.

It was McClure's policy to assign staff members to research and write major articles and series for the magazine, and to Willa soon came one of these assignments. A manuscript had come in on Mary Baker Eddy, founder of Christian Science, and on the "new religion" she espoused. Sam McClure saw in the material possibilities for a series of articles of the type which had made his magazine circulation rocket. He turned it over to Willa to check out the "facts."

This assignment entailed her living for a number of months in Boston, the home of Mary Baker Eddy and of the Mother Church, the First Church of Christ Scientist. Willa took up residence at the old Parker House, where Dickens had often stayed when in America, and went to work.

She found that there were many and strange facts about this astounding woman, Mary Ann Morse Baker Glover Patterson Eddy, which must be carefully checked and authenticated. As she followed up one lead after another, working methodically, she checked off the bits and pieces of information and, in her maturing prose style, began to paint an unforgettable portrait of this woman.

It required all of that year and part of the next for Willa to complete this assignment. As the weeks in Boston stretched into months, she left the Parker House and took a small apartment. And she began meeting people in Boston who were to be important to her writing career. First among them was Ferris Greenslet, who had written an appreciative review of her *April Twilights*. Before meeting in Boston, the two had corresponded. Now he introduced her to friends at Houghton Mifflin, and it was this publishing house that brought out Willa's first four novels.

Another friend she made in Boston opened an equally important door for her—Mrs. Louis Brandeis, wife of the future Justice, who one day said to her, when she had come to call, "Keep on your things. I want to take you . . . to call on a very charming old lady, the widow of James T. Fields." James T. Fields had been a publisher, and his home had long been a rendezvous for authors. So Willa was introduced to the Transcendental literary atmosphere of another era.

Also, this visit led to a meeting with a very dear friend of Mrs. Fields, who was to have an important influence in Willa's career—famed authoress Sarah Orne Jewett. She was present in the Fields' drawing room when Mrs. Brandeis and Willa arrived.

Willa always liked elderly ladies, and they responded to her interest in them. Mrs. Fields was no exception; she liked Willa immediately, and in the seven years of life remaining to her, this first impression did not change.

As much as her friendship with the Brandeises and Mrs. Fields was to mean to Willa, her friendship with Sarah Orne Jewett—even though Miss Jewett had only a little over a year left to live—meant even more. Miss Jewett was not one to give lightly of her friendship, but she was drawn at once to Willa Cather. Though Miss Jewett was twenty-four years Willa's senior and New England through and through, the two had many things in common: Both had come from small towns, were interested in small towns and what had happened to them, were saddened by their decline in vigor and glamour, and used this phenomenon as a subject in their writing. Both loved the countryside around their small towns and had ridden over and over it, absorbing each small detail. Both had known close and satisfying friendships with members of the older generation; both felt that the society of their day was less virile than that of the past. Both were devotees of Flaubert.

Not all of these affinities were discovered upon their first meeting, but the common bond was felt and understood by both women. When Willa left Mrs. Fields' home that day, she felt the elation born of an unusual meeting of minds. However, she did not then dream of the depth and breadth of the influence Sarah Orne Jewett was to have on her own literary career.

Miss Jewett was an artist. She polished her stories endlessly. Furthermore, she wrote from the heart and of things that had been with her for many years.

Her interest in Willa was immediate. She felt sure that she discerned a talent here, but she was not at all satisfied with what its possessor had done with it. She thought Willa no longer young enough for youth to be blamed for what she had not yet done. Miss Jewett had been in poor health for a number of years, ever since an accident in which she had been thrown from a carriage. She was herself very conscious of the fleeting of time. So almost at once she began to exert her influence toward bringing out Willa's artistic best.

Her campaign was two-pronged: to impress upon Willa that the true artist draws on what he knows best and what is dearest to his heart, putting it on paper without artifice; and to help her understand that she must have time and peace and quiet—away from the stimulation and demands of her job at *McClure's*.

Sarah Orne Jewett lived only sixteen months after her first meeting with Willa Cather, and much of that time she and Willa were not simultaneously in Boston. But although the meetings of the two women were comparatively few, correspondence filled in the gaps. Miss Jewett's campaign was carried on with persistence by letter. For example, in one letter, she criticized a story of Willa's, "On the Gull's Road," which had appeared in *McClure's*. She suggested that it might have been better for Willa not to attempt to write from the point of view of a male character, as this was always difficult for a woman. Yet she offered encouragement of a sort by saying that the story "just missed being good."

This was in November, 1908, and following this letter came another in December, probably the climax of Miss Jewett's strategy. In it she singled out "The Sculptor's Funeral" from *The Troll Garden* collection as much superior to the others and at the level of artistry to which Willa must hold.

Miss Jewett died the following June, when Willa was in

England, but the advice she had given her did not die. Most importantly she had written: "Do not hurry too fast. . . . A quiet hour is worth more to you than anything you can do in it. . . . If you don't keep and guard and mature your force, and above all, have time and quiet to perfect your work, you will be writing things not much better than you did five years ago. . . . You must find your own quiet center of life, and write from that to . . . the human heart. . . ."

CHAPTER VII

It was several years before Willa gave up her editorial work at *McClure's* and found her "own quiet center of life" from which to write.

During the years from 1908 through 1912, she went on trips abroad for the magazine, met celebrities, and made a literary name for herself.

After her return from one of these trips, in 1908, she was made managing editor of *McClure's*. Sam McClure had the utmost confidence in her as writer and editor; he trusted her loyalty and integrity. Many who worked with him found him extremely difficult, quarreled with him, and parted from him; but Willa Cather continued to get along with him.

Two other friendships matured during the McClure years. These were with Elizabeth Sergeant and Edith Lewis, both of whom recognized Willa's ability. There was a difference between the two, however, in that Edith Lewis was wholly admiring, while Elizabeth Sergeant was critical of some of her work. Being younger than Willa and less well established in her own writing career, Elizabeth Sergeant was humble but nevertheless frank.

Edith Lewis had met Willa Cather a number of years before their New York association. This meeting had taken place in their native state of Nebraska the summer after Edith Lewis was graduated from college in 1903. She had already read with enthusiasm the columns of dramatic criticism signed "Willa Cather" in the *Lincoln State Journal* and the *Courier,* and had been "enthralled" by them. To her they seemed brilliant. She, too, was interested in writing. She knew Sarah Harris, editor-publisher of the *Courier,* and had mentioned her interest in Willa Cather. So, when Willa was in Lincoln for a few days, Sarah Harris invited both to her home.

As Edith Lewis recalled the first meeting, Willa Cather and Sarah Harris were so deep in some exciting discussion when she arrived that there was only a brief pause while she was introduced; she then became merely a silent, admiring audience.

But when Edith was ready to leave, Willa stood at the door and talked to her for fifteen minutes, questioning her about her aspirations. She seemed impressed by the fact that Edith planned to go to New York soon to live and work, though with no job in view.

The job which Edith Lewis obtained when she reached New York in the fall of 1903 was with the Century Publishing Company. She took a small studio apartment and was thus able to invite Willa to visit her. Willa accepted the invitation the following summer, spending a week of her vacation with Edith. The next summer she spent a longer period of time with her. It was Edith Lewis who had subsequently helped her find the apartment on Washington Square, South.

Shortly after Willa came to New York, a position as editorial proofreader opened on *McClure's Magazine,* and she urged Edith Lewis to apply for it. She obtained the job.

In 1909 the two consolidated their living quarters and took a larger apartment on Washington Place.

Elizabeth Sergeant, on the other hand, did not meet Willa Cather until after Willa had been made managing editor at McClure's in 1908. And she met her in a strictly business, writer-editor situation. Elizabeth Sergeant, a graduate of Bryn Mawr, also had writing aspirations, as well as an interest in social reform. With a letter of introduction from social worker Pauline Goldman and with a manuscript about tenement conditions, Elizabeth Sergeant circled the offices of McClure's, trying to get up enough courage to go in. At last she succeeded. "The only woman I could spy . . ." she said, "coming in my direction was youngish, buoyant, not tall, rather square. . . . This vital being . . . smiled at me, her face, open, direct, honest, blooming with warmth and kindness. Her eyes were sailor blue, her cheeks were rosy, her hair was red-brown, parted in the middle like a child's. . . . Perhaps I did instinctively divine . . . that Willa Sibert Cather was a matchless being —unique in her kind, in her age. I have never in truth met anyone at all like her."

Elizabeth Sergeant's article was accepted by Willa Cather for the magazine, and Elizabeth herself was accepted as a friend.

After spending the following summer in France, Miss Sergeant returned to New York, and one of her first pleasures was a long October afternoon spent with Willa. First there was a ride on the open top deck of a bus to Central Park, then a walk in the Park, following the path to the Reservoir, Willa's favorite walk. The scene had the brilliant colors of October: blue sky overhead, red and gold trees glistening in the sunlight. There was luncheon at Delmonico's, with the head waiter bowing low as his discerning eye took in the luxurious red Liberty gown Miss Cather was wearing, and the table waiter scuttling as she ordered tea that was to be "hot, *hot*, HOT."

Elizabeth Sergeant was enchanted. Truly, she had never known anyone like this editor-author who was like a strong gust of the wind from her Midwest prairies. But in the time that Miss Sergeant had been away, she had read four new stories of Willa Cather's and found them disappointingly imitative of Henry James.

During the luncheon that day in October, Willa told her friend that she planned to give up her editorial position as soon as she could to devote her whole time to writing. Elizabeth hoped this would mean growth.

Willa had learned much at *McClure's* and had met many famous people. Some were intrigued by her; others she antagonized. George Arliss and his wife warmed to her. Edwin Arlington Robinson remained reserved. Mark Twain responded to the vividness and vitality of her nature. Amy Lowell was cold and rude. Through it all, Sam McClure had remained her friend. And he was man enough not to resent it when, late in the fall of 1911, Willa took leave of absence, the first step toward her formal severance from the magazine. She was then almost thirty-eight years old.

In order to have a quiet place to write, Willa, with Isabelle McClung, rented a house in Cherry Valley in Upper New York state, the area from which Isabelle's mother had come. There were relatives and friends to occupy Isabelle while Willa worked, and when Willa laid aside her writing, there was Isabelle to keep her company on long tramps in the country.

The following February, Willa's first novel began to appear serially in *McClure's*. It was titled *Alexander's Masquerade*. Her friend Elizabeth Sergeant read the first installment and was not happy with it. Willa begged her not to read the story piecemeal in the magazine, but to wait and read galley proofs for the book, which Houghton Mifflin was preparing to publish under the title *Alexander's Bridge*.

This Elizabeth did, but still she was disappointed, for the essential ingredient which Sarah Orne Jewett had stressed was missing. Willa had not written from her "own quiet center of life," using her own precious material. Instead, she had written a story about a forty-three-year-old engineer, and had placed him in a sophisticated setting.

At the time of the story, Bartley Alexander was Chief Engineer for the construction of a bridge that was to span the St. Lawrence River. Though he had achieved success in his career and had married well, he felt there was a part of his nature that had never been given a chance. He tried to satisfy what he considered this unfulfilled potential through an affair with an actress. The flaw in his character was symbolized by a flaw in the bridge he was building. Because of faulty figuring in the construction, Alexander's edifice of steel went crashing down, taking with it the man who had conceived it.

The book was imitative—Jamesian in style like a number of Willa's short stories—and contrived. This Elizabeth saw. Despite the fineness of the writing, the story was conventional in plot and structure. None of the characters really came alive. Although there was some valid and interesting psychological probing into Alexander's character, the story was slight.

But because it was sophisticated, another friend of Willa's, Mrs. Fields, was delighted with it. Mrs. Fields had been trying to rub sophistication into the skin of Willa ever since she had met her. Now she felt that she had had some success.

Willa's image as a writer of popular fiction was enhanced by the publication of her first novel, but the book did not bring her recognition as an artist of stature. Nor was she herself ever really pleased with it. In fact, in future years she was publicly deprecatory about it. In an essay, "My First Novels," she wrote:

"*Alexander's Bridge* was very like what painters call a studio picture. It was the result of meeting some interesting people in London. Like most young writers, I thought a book should be made out of 'interesting material,' and at that time I found the new more exciting than the familiar. The impressions I tried to communicate on paper were genuine, but they were very shallow." She called the book "unnecessary and superficial."

Nevertheless, from the time of the publication of *Alexander's Bridge*, it was as an author rather than as an editor that the world was to know Willa Cather, since she did not return to *McClure's*.

She remained at Cherry Valley that fall and early winter, and for the first time wrote something that was pure Cather. It was "The Bohemian Girl," and at last Willa, nearing forty, had found her "own quiet center of life," the life of the Nebraska plains and its immigrant settlers.

53

CHAPTER VIII

Willa sent the manuscript of "The Bohemian Girl" to Elizabeth Sergeant, who saw at once that her friend had finally come into her own. She was so excited that she took the story back in person, in order to share her enthusiasm firsthand. Willa was amazed. She admitted that she herself liked the story, but she had not expected others to care for it. It took some persuading on Elizabeth's part to get her to take it to an editor; she did not think any editor would want it.

But she was wrong. She took the story to Cameron Mackenzie, S. S. McClure's son-in-law, business manager of the magazine. To her surprise, he was enthusiastic about it. He offered her $750 for the story. This she refused, saying $500 was ample; however, she added, with a smile, that perhaps the next story would be worth $750!

Now that she had found she could make her living by writing and realized she had discovered her own milieu, Willa felt a new freedom from tensions. She began to plan a trip West which would be purely vacation—back to Red Cloud to see her parents and on to Winslow, Arizona, to visit her brother Douglass.

Her return to Red Cloud brought mixed reactions. Her old friends, particularly among the immigrants on the Divide, were delighted to see her. But there were others in Red Cloud who thought her arrogant and even rude, some saying she simply could not see them when she walked down the street, others, that she practically elbowed them off the sidewalk.

And as strangely mixed as the feelings of her townspeople

for her were Willa's for Red Cloud and the Divide. When she was away from the stretches of open prairie, she was often nostalgic for them. Yet when she returned, she was often restless and unhappy. On this trip to Red Cloud, she wrote to her friend Elizabeth something of her reaction to the country: The stretches of open country were so vast! She felt as if the very distances would swallow her up. There was no place to hide! Strange, she wrote, that if this country was to be the medium of her art, she was unable to sit down and meditate in it.

Perhaps her preemption of the sidewalk as she strode down the street in Red Cloud was an evidence of rebellion still, as the short hair and boy's clothing had been earlier. And perhaps this rebellion, rather than being against the restrictions of a small Midwest town, was, even in the early days, an involuntary reaction to the prairies' possession of her.

In Arizona it was different. Everything was new to Willa —the people, the scenery, the remains of the Cliff Dwellers' early civilization. With her brothers, when they were children, she had dreamed of exploring the Southwest. Now the dream had come true.

Douglass Cather had lived in the area several years, had done considerable "exploring," and had looked forward to showing his discoveries to his sister. He was employed by the Santa Fe Railroad and had a small house in Winslow, which he shared with another railroad worker named Tooker.

Willa's first impression of Winslow was not favorable. The town was raw and ugly, its refuse piled in disgusting heaps about its perimeter. Willa found it depressing. And her brother's house was as depressing as the town. It was flimsy in construction, unimaginative in design, its interior stark and unattractive. Nor did she care for Tooker. He looked like what she would have liked him to be—strong, open, and frank, a "natural man" without pretensions or artifice. But his conversation was pseudo-intellectual, pseudo-cultural. She took a strong dislike to him, though later she changed her opinion.

But she and Douglass enjoyed each other now as they had when they were children exploring the islands and the banks of the Republican River in Nebraska. And as soon as her brother had an opportunity to begin introducing Willa to the happy Mexicans and his friends among the Indians, she began to enjoy Winslow. She made friends with the people "across the tracks." In particular, she enjoyed their music, and she was soon asked to attend one of their dances.

After the first dance, there were many. Willa was not just a spectator; she was asked to dance and she danced. Larger than her partners and less fleet-footed, she made up for any lack of grace by her happy enjoyment. The smiles which the gaily attired young men in their bright shirts and vests cast her way as she twirled on the dance floor were smiles of genuine friendliness.

Most rewarding of all, however, were the excursions to the Cliff Dwellers' ruins. The first she saw were in Walnut Canyon. Here, walking into the houses of so ancient a people, she felt a link with an American past that went back so far that it seemed to have no beginning. It was a deep and rich experience for Willa.

Soon she and Douglass went on a more extended exploration along the Little Colorado, hunting on their own for more Cliff Dwellings. On this trip, they camped out, and Douglass was able to share with his sister the feeling he had for this country with its rugged, majestic beauty. He was not disappointed in her response.

Willa made no attempt to write while in the Southwest. Besides her interest in the Mexicans and the Cliff Dwellings, she became intrigued with the old Catholic Mission churches that dotted the countryside. Some were deserted and crumbling; others were still in use. They marked the passage of the Missionary Fathers long ago, and they fired Willa's imagination. The passage must have been dramatic, she thought, with much of physical hardship and spiritual struggle. What stories the adobe bricks must harbor!

Fortunately, in making her way about the countryside, Willa had come across a Belgian priest, Father Flatermann, who knew and understood the Indians of the region and had studied the development of the Catholic faith among them. He had eighteen Indian missions under his charge, and he drove from one to another in a spring wagon drawn by a pair of mules. Happily, he was willing to take Willa with him at times and to share his wisdom and knowledge with her. There was nothing sanctimonious about him, and the two found it easy to talk together.

This contact, as well as her whole contact with the Indian Missions, was to be extremely valuable for Willa. From it, though much later, was to come one of her finest novels, *Death Comes for the Archbishop*. She was a person to whom places and the men and women who peopled them were so vivid that their images took up permanent residence in her mind. She was able to live with them in retrospect as fully as she lived in the present.

After two months of the brilliant colors of Arizona and New Mexico, suddenly she had had enough. It was as if, at least for the moment, she had absorbed all she could of their vivid scenes, their people, and their history.

She returned to the East by way of Red Cloud, again stopping for a visit with her father and mother and friends. Nor did she go from there directly to New York. Edith Lewis had given up the apartment she and Willa had shared, so for the moment she had no place to go back to. She stopped off at Pittsburgh with the McClungs, and in the quiet and security of their household, she again took up her pen. She had had enough of vacationing and was eager to get to work.

Much, however, had gotten sorted out in her mind during this long vacation period. It had been well worth the time. She had thrown out the things that were not truly her own, both in the subject matter for her writing and in the

57

form that it would take. In her own words, she had "recovered from the conventional editorial point of view" during her stay in the Southwest. She had succeeded in shedding two shackles: the stimulation of a challenging job and the restrictions it had imposed upon her thinking.

At peace with herself, she began happily working on a book that she thought of as purely for herself. Before her sojourn in Arizona, she had written a story set in Nebraska; she had called it "Alexandra." On her way back, during her visit in Red Cloud, she had seen the wheat harvest for the first time in many years, and another story had taken shape in her mind. She even had a title for it, "The White Mulberry Tree." Now she began putting this story on paper, eagerly, surely.

She wrote only three hours a day, spending the rest of her time with Pittsburgh friends, returning each morning to her work with fresh delight. She was enjoying her writing more than she ever had before. "This was like taking a ride through a familiar country on a horse that knew the way on a fine morning when you felt like riding," she said. And what she was producing was not just a short story, "The White Mulberry Tree," but a novel made up of this story and the earlier one, "Alexandra."

She did not worry about form or arrangement or invention. She was letting the story tell itself. At long last, Willa was walking surely to meet her destiny. She was writing from the quiet center of her being, as Sarah Orne Jewett had counseled her to do.

The book which evolved was *O Pioneers!,* and with it Willa Cather took her place among the literary artists of the early twentieth century.

CHAPTER IX

Willa had returned to the land and its immigrant settlers for the material of *O Pioneers!* In so doing, she had become wholly herself as a writer.

The plot line was simple, depicting the taming of the "wild land" by Alexandra Bergson, a Swedish immigrant. Barely twenty when her father died, she inherited the management of the wide acres he had acquired on the Divide in Nebraska. Though there were three boys in the family, Alexandra's father had believed that she was the one who would have the vision, the courage, and the determination to hold on to the land, should bad times come.

Bad times did come: three successive years of drought and no crops. Though many neighbors left, Alexandra persuaded her brothers not only to stay but to mortgage their farms in order to buy more land. This was a highly successful move, and the Bergsons soon prospered.

Among the neighbors who had given up and moved away were the Linstroms. With their departure, Alexandra lost her one real friend, Carl, a young man near her age. However, her youngest brother, Emil, had something of Carl's understanding nature and sensitivity. On him, she pinned her hopes.

The older boys married, and the Bergson holdings were divided. Alexandra remained on the home place and sent Emil to the University. On the old Linstrom farm now lived a young couple, Marie and Frank Shabata. Marie was gay and full of life, and she and Alexandra developed a satisfying friendship.

Carl Linstrom returned for a visit, and the two older

Bergson boys became concerned lest he marry Alexandra and come into some of the Bergson land. After being belligerently confronted by her brothers, Carl left for the gold fields in Alaska. He would not ask Alexandra to marry him without some substance to offer her.

Emil, home after graduation from the University, fell in love with Marie Shabata, who was estranged from her husband. However, knowing their love to be hopeless, Emil prepared to go away to study law. When he was ready to leave, he stopped to see Marie and found her alone in the orchard. Her husband came home and, discovering the lovers there, shot them.

Alexandra wrote Carl of the tragedy, but received no reply. She was desolate. She went to visit Frank Shabata, now in the penitentiary, and told him she did not blame him, and would exert every effort to have his sentence commuted.

When she returned to her hotel, she found a telegram from Carl. He had returned to Nebraska and was waiting for her.

Carl had done well in Alaska. He and Alexandra planned to be married and he would take her there for the summer—but for the summer only. Then they would return to the Nebraska farm, for Carl understood that Alexandra could never bear to be separated from her land.

The strength of the book lay in its theme—the breaking of the soil—and in Willa's sensitive portrayal of it. In the character of Alexandra she painted not just a strong pioneer type, but a woman with austerity and strength comparable to that of the land she tamed. There were both heroism and pathos in this character. She was a large woman, both in physique and spirit, and her spirit became the spirit of the book.

Critics quibbled a bit about whether the land loomed even larger than the woman as the central character, and some said the book lacked unity. But the reading public, to Willa's surprise, took *O Pioneers!* to its heart.

"*O Pioneers!* interested me tremendously," she said, "because it had to do with a country I loved, because it was about old neighbors. But I did not in the least expect that other people would see anything in a slow-moving story, without 'action,' without a 'hero'. . . ."

But "other people" did.

Near the close of 1912, while Willa was away from the city, Edith Lewis found an apartment which the two would share for fifteen years—as long as the building which housed it stood. Edith must have understood her friend well in order to choose a home which would be so satisfying to Willa that she would do much of her best writing there.

This apartment, too, was in Greenwich Village, but much more spacious than their first. The large rooms, high ceilings, and architecturally good lines pleased both women. The apartment was on the second floor of a large, five-story brick building, constructed originally as a huge single-family dwelling, later converted into ten apartments, two on each floor.

Willa and Edith's apartment had seven rooms, all with big windows and wide window ledges. The rooms were light and airy, with south, east, and west exposures. The walls were thick, shutting out the noise of neighbors and street. Edith knew that Willa was almost fanatical about noise, so in her house hunting, "QUIET" must have hung over her like a placard over a door.

Their new address was Number Five Bank Street.

It was winter when they moved in. There was no central heat in the building, but when adequately fed, large fireplaces furnished ample heat for dining and living rooms. Neither woman was daunted by the necessity of carrying coal to keep the fires going. They were too pleased with their new living quarters to let trivialities interfere with their delight in them. They put down their Oriental rugs, hung curtains, installed the few pieces of furniture they owned, and sallied forth to buy more. They bought solid

61

pieces of mahogany: chests, a round dining-room table, large comfortable chairs. They had open shelves built and filled them with their books. Willa found a large etching of French authoress George Sand, which she bought and hung over the white marble mantel. She explained that she didn't particularly admire George Sand, but thought the etching handsome!

Edith had a nine-to-five job with a publishing house, so shortly after the move to Bank Street, a maid was hired in order that housekeeping duties would not interfere with Willa's writing. She was a real "find," a young French woman, Josephine Bourda, who had been in the United States only a short time. She was quite mistrustful of the strange land and language, so the fine relationship which grew up between her and her new employers was remarkable.

She did not "live in," but came each day from her own home to serve them. She was a splendid cook. This fact was to play a considerable part in the kind of social life which Willa and Edith were able to maintain. Also important were her personality and her ability to manage their home smoothly.

She was full of vitality, was intelligent, and had a good sense of humor. A sincere respect and fine rapport developed between her and Willa. Josephine was to stay with the household during all the Bank Street years.

It was due to her presence that Willa was able to begin having "at homes" on Friday afternoons, when her friends gathered for tea and talk. It was because of Josephine that the two women could begin giving dinner parties with a distinct flavor derived from splendid French cuisine served with Old World elegance.

After Edith went to work in the morning, Willa did the marketing before beginning her stint at the typewriter. She enjoyed this contact with the tradespeople and soon had her favorites among them. The first time Elizabeth Sergeant visited at the new apartment, she went marketing with

Willa. Afterward, she remarked both upon her friend's sensuous enjoyment of the fresh red raspberries and plump, plucked chickens, and upon her camaraderie with the tradespeople. Willa's robust humor, brisk decisiveness, and obvious enjoyment of a shrewd bit of bargaining, brought smiles to the faces of those with whom she dealt. But those whom she did not like she ignored, walking by their stalls as if they were not there. This was a trait of Willa's evident throughout her life. She liked a person, responded to him with enthusiasm and warmth, or she froze and responded not at all. In most cases, if a person once did something that caused her to put up a wall, nothing he might do in the future could dent it.

Willa had always been fond of the opera. There were certain matters which attracted her to it, especially during this period of her life. The color. The drama. But at this time, too, there was someone dynamic, adding to the appeals and the authenticity: Operatic Star Olive Fremstad, who had just come into prominence. Willa became quite enamored of her talent and personality.

Olive Fremstad had been born in Sweden, but had spent her girlhood in Minnesota. Her mother had been a Swedish masseuse, her father, a Norwegian physician. This parentage plus a radical change in the family's way of life when Olive was twelve, added to the difficulties, but probably also to the mystery and power of the singer. The changed living conditions resulted from her father's giving up the practice of medicine in Norway to become a Methodist minister in America. Strangely, he chose the town of St. Peter, Minnesota, a Swedish-Lutheran community, as his destination. One result of this move was such poverty for the family that Olive was thrown completely upon her own resources to obtain a musical education. At one time she was a servant in a Minneapolis home; at another, she was on the music payroll of three churches simultaneously. For her the way to Wagnerian roles and the Metropolitan was long and hard.

Perhaps it was the strength of spirit which had carried Fremstad to her goal that shone forth in her performances and so thrilled and intrigued Willa. Perhaps, too, Willa saw some parallel between her own life and Olive Fremstad's— in their Midwest beginnings and in their determination toward artistic fulfillment.

But the meeting of the two was not auspicious.

Willa still did some writing for *McClure's Magazine,* and about this time she was asked to do an article on the opera. She chose to do it on three operatic stars of the time: Louise Homer, Geraldine Farrar, and Olive Fremstad. She made an appointment with each, but it was the opportunity to meet Olive Fremstad which excited her.

This interview was set for a late-afternoon hour on a day when Willa and Edith and Isabelle McClung, who was visiting them, had tickets for the opera. When Willa arrived at the Fremstad apartment, the star was not there. She had gone for a ride but was expected momentarily. Willa waited, growing nervous at the delay as the appointed time for meeting her friends at the Metropolitan drew closer and closer.

At length, Fremstad arrived, apologetic, and very tired. She looked pale and drawn and old, and her voice was so hoarse she could hardly speak. Willa was amazed, but she was to be even more amazed before the evening was over. She told Fremstad she would return another day and went on to meet her friends at the opera house.

After the three were seated at the Metropolitan, programs for *The Tales of Hoffman* in their hands, Willa hastily told her friends what had happened regarding the Fremstad interview. It was a good thing, she said, that Fremstad was not scheduled to sing that night!

When the first act of the opera was over, the usual intermission lengthened and lengthened. The audience began to grow restless. Surely something had gone wrong, the three friends decided.

It had.

At length, the manager announced that the diva had been taken ill and was unable to continue, but that Olive Fremstad would appear in her place. Willa caught her breath in disbelief.

But when the curtain opened, no worn, drawn, haggard Fremstad appeared, but a beautiful and glamorous creature of seemingly unlimited vitality. She sang superbly, in a voice Willa found it almost impossible to believe was the same she had heard whispering hoarsely two hours before. Her admiration for the star reached new heights.

As time went on, Willa came to know Olive Fremstad well enough so that the two exchanged occasional invitations, but there is no evidence that Fremstad really warmed toward her admirer. However, the singer stirred Willa's imagination to the point where she began planning a book whose main character would be an opera star. She would call it "The Song of the Lark." It would have somewhat the same element of struggle as *O Pioneers!* Willa thought she had seen in Olive Fremstad vision and courage and tenacity akin to that of the immigrant women on the Divide. But how well would she succeed in working with the same theme in a different milieu?

CHAPTER X

If there were those among Willa's friends who were surprised at the turn in her choice of subject matter, there were those also who were disappointed. Although in some respects one knew always what to expect of her—integrity, industry, loyalty—in other respects one did not know at all.

One who felt both surprise and disappointment, though she did not let Willa know it, was Elizabeth Sergeant, recently returned from some months abroad. With the publication of "The Bohemian Girl," then of *O Pioneers!,* Elizabeth had felt sure her friend was on her right and only way. Now as they visited over one of Josephine's excellent meals, she was hearing over and over the praises of this Fremstad —until she grew weary of the name and bored with the eulogies. She was very doubtful of Willa's wisdom in turning to "the artist" for her subject.

Having been separated for a number of months, the two friends, however, had much to say to each other, and met frequently. On these occasions one part of Elizabeth's mind stood off and looked at Willa objectively, seeing her as more of an individualist than ever. She observed her sensuous delight in arranging flowers or dressing lavishly for the opera. She heard her speak in glowing superlatives about people she admired, but in unequivocal tones of disdain about those she did not like. Willa, she decided, was a person whom some would always love and others hate.

Elizabeth watched Willa as she poured tea at one of her early "Friday afternoons," noting that the tea was the same kind as Mrs. Fields had used, and that Willa insisted it be steaming hot. She watched her and understood her concern for her friends, but noted also her inability to become a charming hostess—her inability, even, to be a smooth and polished one. There was something gauche in Willa's movements and her attempts at the social amenities, much as if she were saying, "I want you to enjoy yourselves. Here's your tea. It's hot. Take it and enjoy it. That's all I can do for you."

Her talk was much better after most of the guests had left and only a few of her most intimate friends remained. Then she was more at ease, more herself, more likely to become impassioned about a favorite subject.

When all of the others were gone, then Elizabeth could draw Willa out in talk that really mattered. Was it the foreordained fate of the artist to give up all of the usual fulfillments of life? she asked her. For a woman, the love of a man, the security of being "taken care of," the joys of motherhood?

One's art was enough, Willa replied. In it was fulfillment. Some went one way in life, some another. She had chosen to go the way her Art led her. To be free to do her work was everything.

She resented any intrusions which came as a result of the success of her work, she told Elizabeth. Invitations to join various groups—whether writers' groups or altruistic organizations—she ignored. As she spoke of such invitations and her contempt for the people who sent them, she became another being. Animosity hardened her eyes, stiffened her shoulders, jutted her chin, and sharpened her voice. Inwardly, Elizabeth shuddered. Had she been a more timorous person, she thought, she would have been seriously frightened.

Yet during this time, when *The Song of the Lark* was evolving in Willa's mind, she performed an outstanding act of benevolence for another human being, seeming to belie her attitude toward altruism.

S. S. McClure had finally been ousted completely from his own magazine. He had been forced to sell out and now found himself at loose ends, a state extremely obnoxious to him. He had never been good at writing, yet he wanted to write an autobiography. He felt that his life would interest the reading public, for it had been colorful and stormy; and he felt that it would have something to say to the then "younger generation."

So he came to Willa Cather, seeking help. And he got it. She received him cordially, spent hours on end listening to him reminisce day after day. She took no notes, but each day after he left, she turned to her typewriter. She knew him well. So it was that the story of his life rolled from her typewriter. It was honest; it was forthright. It was McClure and Cather.

The Autobiography of Sam McClure was first run serially in *McClure's Magazine* and later published in book form. Willa made no claim to participation in it, but in his acknowledgments when the book was brought out, Sam McClure included the line: "I am indebted to the cooperation of Miss Willa Sibert Cather for the very existence of this book."

Always Willa seemed to become restless after a period in New York. So now, even though she had taken up her life at Number Five Bank Street with enthusiasm, she was ready to be off for somewhere. In late summer, Olive Fremstad, who had a "camp" in Maine, invited Willa for a visit. Elizabeth had earlier issued an invitation to her summer home. Willa's family were eager to have her visit them in Red Cloud. Douglass and the Southwest had extended tempting invitations. But what she decided upon was to go first to the McClungs' in Pittsburgh, then, with Isabelle, to go back to Virginia and the place of her birth.

Luckily, Isabelle liked walks in the woods; or else she, like Edith, was willing to participate in whatever activities were satisfying to her talented friend. Willa did not find the little town of Gore, her birthplace, much to her liking. Were all small towns depressing? she asked Isabelle. At least, Nature was not. So Isabelle accompanied her on long walks over the beautiful wooded hills of Virginia. Here Willa found regeneration and was soon eager to get back to her desk and the new book that was waiting.

She did not, however, return to New York, but instead went back to Murray Hill in Pittsburgh with Isabelle. Here she worked happily and fruitfully for six weeks. She was always exuberant when her writing was going well, and now it seemed simply to be galloping along. In six weeks, she wrote and rewrote twenty-eight thousand words, a good start on *The Song of the Lark.*

When she returned to New York, she neither saw friends nor accepted telephone calls. She was in a writing frenzy, and did not want it disturbed. If her friends misunderstood her withdrawal, she couldn't help it; this was the way it had to be.

But this was the twelve-month which ushered in 1914.

At first, rumblings from abroad seemed not to concern Willa. She was too immersed in the novel, which was carrying her along at a breathless pace.

In the spring of 1914, however, came a prolonged interruption. She developed a severe scalp infection that put her in the hospital for several weeks, depressing her no end. On her return to the apartment, a lengthy period of convalescence ensued. Even then, she did not feel able to return to work. She felt she needed a change. She decided to go West again.

She stopped off in Pittsburgh, and found herself writing once more, so stayed on for a time. But by midsummer she continued her journey "home" to Red Cloud.

It was here that the news of the Germans marching into Belgium reached her. Still the news, to all outward appearances, was not shattering to her. She went on to make her second visit in the Southwest and did not return to Pittsburgh until late fall.

When she finally did arrive again at Murray Hill, she took up the book where she had left it in summer and continued writing furiously. It went so well that she remained until she had completed it. This was by far the longest book she had written, but because it had pushed her so relentlessly, she was able, despite obstacles and interruptions, to finish it approximately a year from the time it was begun.

Her youngest brother, James, had come back to Pittsburgh with her on her return from Nebraska, to enroll in Carnegie Tech. In order to be with him, Willa stayed on until January of 1915. Then she felt she must get back to where the publishers were and get *The Song of the Lark* into production.

It had been a strange year, in a sense, in that she had written so much in so short a time and been so happy working, even though there had been long delays, personal difficulties, and world upheaval. It was a year which only the future could evaluate.

CHAPTER XI

By 1915, Willa Cather was apparently thinking of herself as an artist with a "mission," a personage who might indulge her eccentricities. Problems did not make her more reasonable.

She was unhappy and difficult while reading proofs of *The Song of the Lark.* And she was made no less downhearted when the British publisher, William Heinemann, who had published *O Pioneers!* in England, turned down the new book. She had great respect for Heinemann and his discriminating taste in literature. So she was deeply hurt by his rejection of her latest novel. He sent her a handwritten note explaining his rejection, saying that he felt Miss Cather had employed a method which was not natural to her, telling "everything about everybody." It was a type of writing which he felt to be "distressingly familiar."

When she was through with the proofs of *The Song of the Lark,* Willa was again ready to be off. It was the summer of 1915, and *McClure's Magazine* would have liked her to go abroad for them; she considered it, contacted Isabelle McClung to see if she might accompany her, but decided against the trip when Judge McClung refused to let Isabelle go to war-infested Europe. Instead, Willa began planning another trip to the Southwest, this time with Edith Lewis.

The two women shopped for khakis, boots, and cowboy hats, for Willa knew they needed to be equipped for "roughing it." This time she wanted to include a visit to the Mesa Verde in Southeastern Colorado, a place which had long interested her.

They left New York by train, going first to Chicago, then

to Denver, and finally to Mancos, Colorado. This was the closest depot to the Mesa Verde. Here Willa immediately made it known that she wished to locate a member of the Wetherill family (It was a Wetherill boy who had discovered the Mesa Verde about thirty years before.); and that she wished to find a team and driver who would take her and her friend to the Mesa.

In both, she succeeded. She found that a brother of Dick Wetherill was still living in Mancos and made an evening appointment with him. He enjoyed telling the story of his brother's monumental discovery, and he told it well: how Dick Wetherill, looking for stray cattle, swam the Mancos River on his horse and rode up and up until he reached the "green tableland" some two thousand feet above the valley —a vast level summit of an abrupt uprising from the plain. He had found it to be covered with low-growing junipers and piñon trees, like a thick beard on a jutting chin. On closer inspection, he had also discovered that there were great swaths cut through the green beard, as if by a giant razor. As he rode closer to one of these swaths, he saw it was a deep canyon with precipitous walls of clay. On the far wall, which lay bathed in sunlight, something caught his eye.

Curious, he decided to investigate. From a distance, he received the impression that there was a huge cave opening in the wall. As he made his way down the rugged slope to the canyon floor, he saw that he had been right and that the cave seemed to be subdivided. By the time he had reached the bottom, he was filled with a tremendous excitement, and as he explored the "cave," he knew with certainty that people had lived in it; that, in fact, half buried by fallen rock and overgrown with the persistent juniper, here lay the ruins of a village of some ancient people.

To hear the story of the discovery of these dwellings of an ancient civilization was almost as exciting to Willa as the actual discovery must have been to young Dick Wetherill.

The next morning, as Willa and Edith set out on the

rough twenty-mile drive to the Mesa, their anticipation electrified the air. Much of the small town's citizenry turned out to watch them climb aboard the wagon. The observers found the proceeding novel, interesting, and a bit amusing.

Due to the remoteness of the Mesa Verde Park and the difficulty of access, few tourists visited it in 1915. The advent of two women, alone, was indeed an innovation. However, the young forester's assistant, "Jeep," who received them, offered himself as their guide. He took them on various expeditions and was able to devote his time and attention almost exclusively to them until the next-to-last day of their visit.

On the last day of their stay, it had been planned that Jeep would take them to an unexcavated ruin known as "The Tower House," but another party of tourists had arrived the day before, demanding his attention. So he enlisted his brother-in-law, a man named Richnor, to act as the ladies' guide.

The three set out, with Richnor plodding ahead and his charges following after. Questions asked of this guide gained scant response. The rapport Willa had had with Jeep was not forthcoming with Richnor.

When they reached Soda Canyon, Richnor said tersely that they must descend to the floor and that by following it they would come to the Tower House Ruins. The trail down which he led them was both difficult and hazardous. At times it was necessary to cling to scraggly junipers on one ledge, then drop to the ledge below. Richnor offered no help. He simply went ahead and expected the women to follow. Like mountain goats, the three scrambled down the precipitous rock wall. Miraculously, he did get his charges, though disheveled and breathless, safely to the canyon floor. Then they set out "Indian style" along the bottom of the canyon. After a while, Willa began addressing pertinent questions to Richnor's back: How were they to get back up that cliff face without ropes?

He would take them back up by another trail, he replied with a shrug.

How far did they still have to go to reach the ruins?

Well, it was quite a little piece. They couldn't spend much time at the ruins. They'd have to get out before dark.

But what she had come for was to see the ruins, Willa reminded him.

She'd see them, he responded.

After a considerable hike down the canyon, she did see them. Richnor sat on a rock resting, while the women explored. By midafternoon, he insisted that they had to go.

For several hours, he led them on down the canyon. The walking was good, the floor of the canyon smooth and grass-covered and the weather fair, so no caustic comments came from the rear.

Finally, when they reached a point at which another canyon branched off from the one they were in, Richnor stopped. With no great show of concern, he admitted that he didn't know where the trail was that he had been seeking. Maybe they'd passed it. He thought there was an archeologists' camp four or five miles up Cliff Canyon, to which they had just come. Maybe they should go that way.

Willa objected, for obvious reasons. He was not sure where the archeologists' camp was located and might well be leading them on another unfruitful five-mile hike. He responded with a grunt, followed by a silence which said plainly, "Then what do you suggest?"

Willa had a suggestion: that he go on alone to try to find the camp, while they waited at the intersection of the two canyons until he could find a way to get them out.

There was a large, flat rock nearby. Willa and Edith sat there to rest and wait. They were not alarmed, for they felt sure they would be found.

The wait stretched through the twilight hours and into the night. The friends talked little as they watched the dramatic changes of color, of light and shadow, as day faded and night took over.

It was four or five hours before they heard shouts from Cliff Canyon, reassuring them that help was on the way. Soon two men from the Fewkes' Camp arrived to lead them out. Richnor had not returned with them. He had arrived at the camp exhausted.

It was two o'clock in the morning when the party reached the archeologists' camp. A team of horses was hitched up and the women were driven back to their own quarters.

It was an extremely short night. At eight o'clock the same morning, the team and driver came from Mancos, as per previous agreement, to take them back to town.

After resting for a few days, Willa and Edith went on to Taos, New Mexico, where they stayed for a month, boarding with a Mexican woman in an adobe "hotel." They rode about the countryside daily, either on horseback or behind a rented team, which they themselves drove. The Mexicans, asked for directions, gave Willa careful instructions for finding her way to the little churches and other landmarks.

Earlier impressions of the Southwest had been used in *The Song of the Lark.* Those gleaned at this time would be grist for future mills.

CHAPTER XII

Some have the artistic gift, but few also have the artistic "passion." Thea Kronborg, the main character of *The Song of the Lark*, was one of those rare creatures, dedicated as well as endowed.

She was born the sixth of seven children to a minister and his wife in the village of Moonstone, Colorado. She showed a musical aptitude at an early age, practiced four hours a day, and took piano lessons from Professor Wunsch, a dissipated German wanderer. Soon after he left Moonstone, Thea dropped out of high school and began teaching music pupils of her own. She had finished and furnished her own loft hideaway and there read nightly and mused about the stars and the universe.

Two men had a deep influence upon her life even then. One was Ray Kennedy, a kindly, thirtyish railroader, whose designs for material wealth were either fostered a little too early or a little too late to be successful. He had watched Thea grow and had long planned to marry her when the proper time came.

Dr. Archie, the town doctor, unhappily married, was an understanding friend. After Ray Kennedy had been killed in a train accident, it was Dr. Archie who accompanied Thea to Chicago where she was to live and take piano lessons, using for this purpose six hundred dollars Ray had bequeathed her. Dr. Archie saw to it that Thea was pleasantly established in the home of two widows, a mother and her daughter; that she was scheduled to take piano lessons from Harsanyi, the finest piano teacher in the city; and that she was to be soloist in a church choir to supplement her six-month stipend.

Through something of a fluke, Harsanyi found that Thea's voice held far more promise than her fingers. He succeeded in getting her placed as accompanist-secretary in the studio of a renowned voice teacher.

The male chain of influence upon Thea continued in Fred Ottenburg, scion of a brewery family and a patron of music. He, in turn, introduced her to other wealthy, cultured patrons.

But Thea was in a personal and professional lethargy. Ottenburg convinced her that an expense-paid vacation alone in the Southwest would be the remedy. There Thea became enthralled with the Cliff Dwellers' country and found this experience a catalizing agent for her own inner core of artistic determination.

Fred arrived in Panther Canyon. Thea and Fred fell in love. After a time, they traveled to Mexico, then to New York.

Fred Ottenburg was married and Thea refused to be his mistress. She was certain that intensive study in Germany was a necessity. Though Ottenburg would have financed it, she appealed to Dr. Archie, who had invested in a prolific mine and was then residing in Denver. He went to New York, loaned her the money, and, with Fred, saw her ship depart.

The story picked up ten years later with Thea, Fred, and Dr. Archie all in New York again. Thea, a Wagnerian star, no longer needed individual approbation or encouragement; she had long since become single-purposed in her career. The two men, then, acted simply as foils to whom she sounded her artistic and personal credo.

The book was an admixture of Olive Fremstad and Willa Cather. Fremstad did show musical talent when very young, did have a struggle, was sponsored by wealthy families in the Twin Cities, did work and study in a New York studio, and did rise to tremendous operatic heights. But it was Willa Cather who, as a girl, had had that precious cool and cold garret. Association with cultured Germans and with doctors in her home town had been Willa's privilege. Willa had felt deeply about the Southwest. Thea's summer in Moonstone, after her first months in Chicago, was much like that of Willa's in Red Cloud after she had been East— the awareness of an artistic temperament's aloneness in a somewhat rough environment, and the realization that she and her friends had formed vastly different attitudes and values.

The epilogue of *The Song of the Lark* concerned Moonstone legends about Thea. This situation was much like that in St. Peter, Minnesota, where little remains of Olive Fremstad except legend.

When *The Song of the Lark* appeared, it was not met with the reader enthusiasm with which *O Pioneers!* had been received. Fewer readers could identify with the struggling opera star than with the pioneer woman of the previous book. The story was conventional in structure and plot. Some thought the male characters were not convincingly masculine; others, that the book was too long and continued a hundred and fifty pages after the climax had been reached.

The overuse of detail was felt by the novelist herself. When she revised the book for reissue in 1932, she cut nearly one-tenth of the text. Even in its revised form, however, she remained critical of the book in later years. Never again did she use "the friendly, confidential tone of writing" to which William Heinemann had objected.

It was news of the serious illness of Willa's mother that brought the Cather-Lewis sojourn in the Southwest to an abrupt end in the summer of 1916. Edith went back to New York and her job, but Willa went to Red Cloud to help care for her mother.

She had wired from the Southwest that she would soon be home to "take over." The relationship between mother and daughter had never been entirely harmonious, for both were strong-willed and strong-minded. Now, weakened by her illness, Mrs. Cather no doubt had some trepidation about her household's being taken over by Willa, especially a Willa who was now used to having a French maid to handle her own household tasks. Mr. Cather had purchased a house, one considerably larger than the rented one of Willa's childhood.

Nonetheless, when Willa rolled up her sleeves and attacked the wood-burning range to prepare delicacies for her parents and substantial dishes for the rest of the family—even, after a time, homemade bread—Mrs. Cather was happy to have her.

Mr. Cather was always pleased with Willa's companionship. Now he glowed in her presence. He understood his eldest daughter as a person and as a writer, probably better than any other member of the family.

After Mrs. Cather was better, Willa went calling. Annie Pavelka, who had been the Miners' hired girl when Willa was little, was first on her list.

As a child, Willa had always been fascinated by Annie, who was full of vitality and was always doing something interesting. Willa remembered how she would borrow Mrs. Miner's sewing machine in those days and make herself stunning dresses, copied from those of the "elite" young ladies of the town. She had even made herself everyday shoes, for her entire salary of eighteen dollars a month went to her family, living in a dugout on the Divide. And while Mrs. Miner had seen to it that Annie was kept in a pair of shoes "for good," Annie would not wear these to work in. They must be kept shining for the dances which she loved to attend. So Willa, with the Miner children, had watched Annie stitch cardboard insoles between oilcloth and denim, then attach cloth "uppers" and strong black tapes with which to tie on the shoes.

Eventually, Annie had married a Bohemian youth. They had settled on the Divide, raised a large and fine family, and here they still lived. When Annie heard that "Miss Willie" was home that summer, she sent word that Willa must come out to the farm and visit them. She wanted her boys to get acquainted with her old friend. And she wanted Miss Willie to come for a meal.

Willa promised and at last sent word that she would be there on a certain day. Annie set about making *kolaches* and banana cream pie, and giving her big sons all kinds of directions and instructions so they would know how to act.

But they really didn't need their mother's admonitions. All their lives they had been hearing about Willie Cather and had at various times met her briefly. They were well indoctrinated with the idea that she was someone very special, and always had been. Willa was the most inquisitive child anybody ever saw, their mother had told them. She was all eyes and ears. And then, too, Miss Willie had always been kind to Annie.

Annie's face grew flushed with her preparations for the great occasion. She was doing for her good friend, and she was happy.

Most important of all, the coffee must be boiling hot when it was poured, for she remembered how, ever since Willa had been grown, she'd had no use for tea or coffee unless it was so hot that most other people couldn't drink it.

Later Willa said that she "had always wanted to write a book about Annie," but it was during this summer of 1916 that the book which was to be *My Antonia* took shape in her mind. She was in Red Cloud several months, and before she departed she had begun working on the early chapters of this book.

Back in New York in the fall, she went to have tea with Elizabeth Sergeant in her apartment near Central Park. While Elizabeth made the tea, Willa picked up a bright orange-and-blue apothecary jar which was filled with flowers and set it in the middle of a round, bare table. She said to her friend that she wanted the heroine of her next book to be like this vase on the table, a rare object which could be viewed from all sides. Elizabeth, always careful not to initiate a conversation about what Willa was working on, allowed herself the privilege of one soft-spoken question: Someone Willa had known when she was a child, perhaps? Willa nodded, and Elizabeth said no more.

It was only a few weeks later that Elizabeth and Willa were walking together in Central Park, conversing briskly. Suddenly Willa announced that her good friend Isabelle McClung was going to be married.

Elizabeth was surprised at the announcement but not at the bleakness of Willa's tone and face. Judge McClung had died the preceding fall. Elizabeth knew that Willa was feeling as if a rug had been jerked from under her feet. Isabelle was marrying a violinist, Jan Hambourg, whose work as a concert artist would mean a life of almost continuous travel. There was no other home comparable to Murray Hill that could serve as a haven for Willa Cather. Somehow she always seemed to need a place away from New York in which to write, for at least a part of each year, she said.

Might her own old home in Red Cloud be the answer? No, she had never been able to write in Nebraska, she said.

This strange phenomenon seemed to stem from one of two things: the unfavorable reaction of a large segment of the community to Willie, the teen-age maverick, which she still resented; or the strong hold which the country itself had upon her, against which she seemed instinctively to fight. Whichever it was, it seemed to spring from something in Willa Cather's nature which rebelled against any type of personal bondage, and she was becoming increasingly aware that her time and energy must be husbanded.

She must find some sanctuary.

CHAPTER XIII

The public saw less and less of Willa Cather as time went on; her publishers, more and more. Her "Friday afternoons" were discontinued. The war offered a good excuse, but the more casual of her acquaintances felt there was another reason—that Willa Cather was feeling her importance and couldn't be bothered with lesser mortals. Although friends knew there was some truth in this, they, more tolerant, ascribed her isolation to the fact that she must save herself for her work.

The novel which was to be *My Antonia* progressed apace after Willa returned to New York in the late fall of 1916. This time she had little to say about the story on which she was working, other than that it was "the story of Annie on the Divide" and that she was letting the story take her where it would. Elizabeth Sergeant noted the difference. Before, Willa had seemed to want reassurance and encouragement as she worked. Now she seemed not to need it. Elizabeth wondered hopefully if her friend had finally reached a point of maturity in her writing where she had confidence in what she was doing.

There was something else Elizabeth noticed about Willa at the time—her apparent desire to shut the war out as if it did not exist. Was this too a means of protection, protection against becoming involved emotionally? Or was she so engrossed in her writing that it simply crowded out all else? Possibly to become what she was becoming, a major novelist, she had to be egocentric.

At any rate, Willa still found it necessary to get out of New York periodically, and as the McClung mansion was no longer an available refuge, she must find another. Fortunately for her, in the summer of 1917, two of her women friends from Pittsburgh rented a lovely house, "High Mowing," just outside of Jaffrey, New Hampshire, where they invited her to visit them.

Willa was charmed with this spot in New England. The area was almost entirely new to her. Only when she was researching the Mary Baker Eddy biography for Sam McClure had she lived in New England. Then most of her time had been spent in the city of Boston. Hence this was a new experience of "place," and places were always of great importance to her.

There were a number of charming inns in the vicinity. One, only a few miles from High Mowing, was The Shattuck. Here, in this large, white-frame, four-story inn, with its quiet dignity and New England gentility, Willa was to find the new sanctuary she was seeking. Her friends from High Mowing took her there when she expressed a desire to find a place to work for the rest of the summer. The Shattucks, who owned the inn at the time, had previously met the ladies from High Mowing and so accepted Willa without question. She engaged two small rooms on the top floor, facing Mount Monadnock. She requested privacy, and her request was respected. Her name did not appear on the register in 1917 or in subsequent years.

So began a long and pleasant association between Willa and the inn and its proprietors. They reserved the rooms under the eaves for her for a number of years, and treated her well. But they paid little attention to her renown as an author. After she had been coming there for several years, their daughter Eleanor, then in Wellesley College, was handed a book of Willa Cather's and told it was on "the required reading list." Eleanor exclaimed in surprise, "Why, she stays at our Inn!"

That first summer Willa was at Jaffrey, the Hambourgs —Isabelle McClung and her husband of recent date— joined her at Shattuck. In them and the Misses Hine and

Acheson from High Mowing, she had her own small coterie. She kept aloof from the other Inn guests, who generally saw her only at meals. The permanent guests, chiefly little old ladies, observed her with interest, for she was "different." She appeared at breakfast in middy blouse and skirt and sturdy walking shoes, and if she did not actually "stride" in, she came close to it. She walked as if she were going somewhere and intended to get there. She was present for breakfast every morning rather early, ate heartily, and demanded that her coffee be *hot*. She did not loiter over her food, but ate in haste as a boy might do his chores before going hunting.

Few of the guests knew she was engrossed in the writing of *My Antonia*.

During the hot summer days, she worked away from the Inn. Her friends at High Mowing had pitched a tent in their meadow for her. Each morning after breakfast she made briskly for this spot, manuscript and writing materials in hand. She left by the back door of the Inn, so only the staff saw her go. She walked the half mile through the woods, often finding the dew still damp on the pine needles and lady's slippers. The tent was sparsely furnished, containing only a table and camp chair. Here, completely alone, with the scent of pines and wild flowers brought to her by the summer breeze, she worked contentedly and fruitfully.

The personnel at the Inn found it easy to keep her room, since she was gone most mornings. And her things were always put neatly away. The only times they found her difficult were when delays in the kitchen detained her meals— and when her coffee was not steaming hot.

The townspeople the first summer Willa was at Jaffrey saw almost nothing of her. Occasionally, she visited the village hairdresser, who thought it a little strange that the appointments were not made in Willa Cather's name, but in the name of the friend who called. Did this Miss Cather think she was so famous that people would flock to the beauty parlor just for a look at her?

The Hambourgs left, and as fall came on, Willa was ready to return to New York and Number Five Bank Street. Her Pittsburgh friends were going home, but would be coming back to High Mowing the following summer. It had been a good summer for Willa. As a matter of fact, she had completed Book II of *My Antonia* while at Jaffrey. She was halfway through the novel.

During the following winter, she finished the book. And the next summer, the summer of 1918, she returned to Jaffrey and the Shattuck Inn. This time Edith Lewis accompanied her. Together, they read the proofs of *My Antonia*.

The little old ladies found Willa a bit more sociable the second summer. Sometimes after lunch or dinner she would sit down and visit with them. She seemed to be interested in what they were thinking and what they had to say. They liked the attention she gave them.

Concerts were presented from time to time in the evening in the Shattuck parlors. Willa attended these, but did not remain downstairs for other activities such as card games.

Occasionally some of the ladies would catch a glimpse of Willa and Edith out of doors during the morning hours. Usually they were en route to some wooded spot, carrying papers and pencils. When they found a suitable rock or fallen log for a seat, they took up their work on the proofs.

Edith thought this was a particularly enjoyable summer, partly because of the lovely New England woods in which they often worked, and partly because Willa was less tense than she usually was when reading proofs. Paradoxically, however, she felt that Willa was being extremely critical of her own writing. She cut where she felt a passage was not sufficiently economical. She rewrote sentences, even paragraphs at times, making radical changes—changes which Edith thought were always to the good. For these, her publisher would have to be paid, because they meant more work for the typesetter.

So the proofs of *My Antonia* were corrected and returned to Houghton Mifflin, and in the fall the book came off their presses. It was one of the finest she was to write. Though she would later develop more finesse and economy of style, she would never surpass the artistic naturalness and beauty of *My Antonia*.

Like *O Pioneers!*, it was a simple story of immigrant settlers in Nebraska. But this time it was about a Bohemian family, the Shimerdas, and, chiefly, their daughter Antonia. The story was told by a neighbor boy, Jim Burden, who became Antonia's good friend.

Mr. Shimerda was a violinist, a cultured, sensitive man, who had been driven to leave his homeland by a wife greedy for land for their son Ambrosch. There was a second son, Marek, mentally retarded, and a little girl younger than Antonia. When the Shimerdas arrived at the farm they had bought sight unseen, they found only a cave for living accommodations.

Antonia was a gay, intelligent girl, sensitive alike to the country about her and to its inhabitants. She was very close to her father. But Mr. Shimerda could not bear the bleak and barren life to which they had come. He shot himself before the first winter was over.

From then on, Ambrosch forced his sister Antonia to work in the fields like a man. This coarsened her, and she seemed to become more like her boastful, arrogant brother. However, an opportunity arose for her to work in the nearby town of Black Hawk as a "hired girl," and her brother agreed to this because of the wages she could send home.

In town, Antonia lost the crude ways she had been acquiring. She learned to cook and sew—and to dance. With the other country girls who worked in town, she went to every dance. At one she met Larry Donovan, a train conductor who spent his free time in Black Hawk. She fell in love with him and went to Denver to meet and marry him. Instead of marrying her, he deserted her. She returned home, had a baby, and again began working for her brother Ambrosch.

The last section of the book took up the story twenty years later. Jim Burden, who had become a successful New York lawyer, came back to see Antonia. She had married Anton Cuzak, of her own nationality, and borne ten more children in the intervening years. By hard work, they had paid for a large and productive Nebraska farm, where they now lived.

Jim found to his delight that Antonia had not changed, except outwardly. There was in her eyes the same zest for life. He enjoyed meeting her husband and her children. He saw at once that they were a wonderful family—the imprint of Antonia's strong and lively personality plain upon them. He was content. The years had not dimmed the essence of the vivid young girl who had been his playmate. She was still his Antonia.

A mere summary of the plot of this novel cannot even hint at the strength and pull of the story. These lie in the beautifully vivid descriptions of the prairie; in the personality of Antonia, who comes so alive in the pages; in the spirit of genuineness that pervades the book; and in the true values which it presents. *My Antonia* is a sensitive and beautiful story. It is in this book that there occurred the unique, striking image and symbol of the plowshare against the setting sun: ". . . a plough had been left standing in the field. The sun was sinking just behind it. Magnified . . . by the horizontal light, it stood out against the sun—black against the molten red. There it was, heroic in size, a picture writing on the sun . . ."

Willa had drawn many of her characters from childhood friends and neighbors: The Miner family, who had lived next door to the Cathers, became the Harlings for whom Antonia worked in town. Antonia herself was patterned on Annie Pavelka who remained a lifelong friend of Willa's.

And Jim Burden, the narrator, simply substituted for the eyes of "Willie Cather," through whom the story really was told. Again, this was her own material, and she had written from the center of her being. So she had been able to capture the spirit of the plains and the pioneers who peopled them. "Like a fabric loosely yet carefully woven, *My Antonia,* is made," another writer, Nora Lewison, was to say of it, "made rough in texture, rich and warm in color; made by a workman sincere and skilled."

It was the best book Willa Cather had written thus far, but it was the last book of Willa Cather's to be initially published by Houghton Mifflin.

CHAPTER XIV

Ferris Greenslet, the member of the Houghton Mifflin staff who was always most enthusiastic about Willa's books, had been excited about *My Antonia*; the partners themselves had been less so. The book did not sell as well as Willa thought it should, and this she attributed to the lack of enthusiasm by the publishers, the drab book jacket they had chosen for it, and inadequate advertising. Her dissatisfaction resulted in her seeking another publisher.

Some of her friends who thought she had "shut out" the war were surprised to learn that, having finished *My Antonia*, she immediately embarked on a novel with a war theme. Nonetheless, she remained most unhappy about the conflict in Europe, unsympathetic toward it, and pessimistic as to its outcome. There were those who considered her unpatriotic because of this attitude.

Her closest friends knew of a personal loss the war had brought her: the death of a favorite young cousin during the first American offensive. They knew there had been an affinity between the cousins such as Willa had experienced with few persons. Now she was working on a book which they understood had a World War I setting and involved a hero suggested by her cousin. By her own account, this was going to be a long book. She was going back to Jaffrey to work on it the summer of 1919.

When the Shattucks received word that she was returning to the Inn for the third summer, certain accouterments were to be brought out for "Miss Cather's rooms." This provoked smiles, but they were tolerant smiles. There was the heavy coil of rope that must be carried to the fourth floor and secured at her window. (Willa Cather was as fearful of fire as Hans Christian Andersen, who always carried a rope "fire escape" with him on his journeys.) The other accessories, which they had to get out of storage and put on the line to air, were heavy black cambric draperies with which to shut out the view when she worked in her room. These she herself had purchased.

The maids, who hung the drapes shortly before Willa was to arrive, giggled at their ugliness and agreed they were glad they didn't have a job that required shutting out the view of the mountain. Most of the guests came to Jaffrey specifically to enjoy this view.

Willa's tent was again pitched in the High Mowing meadow so that she could work outdoors when she chose. And even though there was considerable rain and much damp weather that summer, she chose to go there most mornings. The other guests shook their heads as they watched her venturing out in the mist and dampness. Their concern proved to be justified. She ventured once too often and caught a severe cold.

The cold did not improve even though the Shattucks persuaded her to stay in her room instead of continuing to go to the tent. In fact, her condition grew worse, and she developed a badly infected throat. The Shattucks suggested that they call Dr. Frederick Sweeney, who came frequently to attend guests at the Inn. Willa agreed, and Dr. Sweeney was called.

The doctor was pleased to have an opportunity to meet and visit with Willa Cather. On his calls, he sat by her bedside and chatted. He had diagnosed her illness as influenza, and during one of their conversations, he mentioned that he had combated a large-scale influenza epidemic on an American troopship between New York and Saint Nazaire, France. When Willa expressed interest in the troopship, he told her he, had kept a diary during his time as a medical officer. Willa explained that she was working on a book with an American soldier as hero, and that she had been wondering how she was going to "get him to France." Dr. Sweeney was not surprised when she asked if he would consider lending her the diary. He agreed to bring it the next time he called.

She did make use of it, as he was to see when *One of Ours* was published. Again a medical doctor had helped shape Willa Cather's work.

When Willa returned to New York that fall, she continued zealously working on *One of Ours*. But Edith Lewis noted that she was not pleased with Houghton Mifflin and, knowing her friend well, was quite sure that Willa would do something about it.

She did. One afternoon early in the spring of 1920, a young man named Alfred A. Knopf, quite new to the publishing business, was sitting in his office, a partitioned-off corner of the nineteenth floor of the Chandler Building on West Forty-second Street. One of the shipping clerks in the outer room knocked on his door and said there was a lady to see him; her name was Willa Cather. Knopf knew the name, he knew her publisher, and he knew her books.

He did not flatter her, however, as they talked together. Nor did he try to sell her on the merits of his firm. By his attitude, he almost dared her to laugh at him when she inquired about some blue binding paper on his desk and he explained that it was for a book of Chinese poetry and that he had gone to the Metropolitan Museum of Art to find just the shade of Chinese blue he wanted. But as their conversation progressed, he could see that he need not have been afraid of her laughing at a man's hunting "just the right shade of blue" for binding a book of Chinese poetry. He saw that her taste, too, was discriminating, and that she admired the care he was giving the books his firm was publishing.

He was not surprised when she asked him if he would care to be her publisher. He was, however, not ready to give her an answer. His taste was as discriminating in regard to the text of a book as to the paper it was to be printed on or its binding. He thought he would like to do business with the author of *My Antonia*. Still, he said he thought it best they both think the matter over, reminding Willa that changing publishers was a very serious business. He invited her to come back at a later time. He felt quite sure she would, and he was not mistaken.

At this second meeting, he was ready to agree that they try a publishing venture together if she had something to submit. He had observed her carefully, and he thought that, although she might not be the easiest person in the world to do business with, she would offer him a worthwhile challenge.

As she was only about two-thirds of the way through *One of Ours* at this time, Willa said she had nothing to offer him unless he would be interested in bringing out a collection of her short stories. He thought this would be a good beginning.

A few months later the collection entitled *Youth and the Bright Medusa* was published by the Alfred A. Knopf Company. The collection included four previously published stories and four new ones. Willa had done some sharp revision of the older stories, and they, as well as the new ones, were beginning to show the conciseness and economy which became characteristic of her style.

While working on *One of Ours,* Willa entertained more than she had in a long time, her guests mostly returned soldiers. Often three or four or a half dozen of them would come together, and remain long over tea, talking, reminiscing about their war experiences, and answering the questions put by Willa.

But now she said she had done all she could on the book until she could spend some time in France, for the last section of the book was to be laid abroad. Edith Lewis took a long leave of absence from her job and devoted the summer and fall of 1920 to being the companion of her friend in Paris. Living on the Left Bank, Willa "transported" herself —and Edith admits to having been "transported" with her

—back to the Middle Ages. She had reason for this. She wanted to get the feel of France, not only as it was in 1920, but even more to understand its past, to know what had gone into the making of it. Edith, too, found pleasure in living in this re-created world. She did not go out on her own to enjoy the Paris of bright lights and beautiful shops, but spent her time with her friend; they seldom left the sector between the Seine and the Luxembourg Gardens. They went beyond the Tuileries on the Right Bank to attend the Opéra Comique a few times; that was all.

Many of Willa's friends had given her the names and addresses of people whom they wanted her to meet while she was in Paris, but they were disappointed upon her return to discover that she had neither looked them up nor called them.

After six or seven weeks of living "in the Middle Ages," however, Edith left Willa to go to Italy. Jan Hambourg, Isabelle's husband, had suggested that he would be glad to guide Willa on a tour of the World War I battlefields in France, and this he now did. His knowledge of the language, the country, and the French people was excellent. He was glad to use it to help his wife's friend. Thus Willa became acquainted with the more recent as well as the older aspects of French history, both of which she needed for *One of Ours.*

In August, Edith and Willa met again in the south of France. Though Willa was eager to return home, at Edith's urging, she agreed to remain in France until October.

One of Ours was completed that winter in New York. It was the first novel of Willa Cather's to be published by Alfred A. Knopf. It reached the bookshops in September of 1922, sold well, and brought its author the greatest financial reward she had yet known. It also won the Pulitzer Prize.

CHAPTER XV

One of Ours had to do with a man who found himself. At least he thought he had found himself.

Claude Wheeler was born and took his proper place on a Nebraska farm. He did all the proper things including hoeing, harvesting, and marrying.

But Claude was an idealist. It was not until World War I, his enlistment, and time in France that it seemed to him he was in his true place. He dreamed of remaining in France, buying a small farm and working it. Fighting for a cause in which he believed was his niche; the farm in France would be his niche.

However, Claude Wheeler was killed on the line, as was his best friend, an American violinist whom he had met in the army. Claude had sought in Nebraska for someone to admire wholeheartedly, but had not found such a person until he reached France. Fighting for a cause to which he had given himself and having found a friend whom he loved and admired, he died an idealist fulfilled.

Willa Cather's projection was remarkable. Having never been immediately in war circumstances, she was still able, through intelligence and empathy, to re-create the war scenes and communicate them so that her readers lived them. It was a romantic story and it idealized war. The book was understandably popular in the 1920's. Its author was not alone in idealizing war at the time. "The war to end war" and "making the world safe for Democracy" were popular slogans of the day.

During much of Willa's writing career, her works received more attention from English critics than from American. This was not true, however, with *One of Ours*. At the time of its publication, it was hailed at home as well as abroad with high praise and called her best book. But time was to sober this general exuberance of reviewers and critics. In fact, there were a few dissenters even in the beginning. Novelist Sinclair Lewis, for example, usually a staunch Cather supporter, said he thought it doubtful the war scenes should have been brought into the book at all; that they did not seem an integral part of it.

Later critics considered *One of Ours* far from Willa Cather's best book. One, Maxwell Geismar, wrote in 1943: "There is no doubt that *One of Ours* . . . is Cather's weakest novel up to this point."

Critics with hindsight have said that in *One of Ours* the pessimism which was to obsess Willa because of the machine age and its evils was beginning to show; that in this novel the machine was a symbol of a new kind of society which was not to her liking.

Willa Cather has often been quoted as saying later, with hindsight too, that in the 1920's "the world broke in two." But at this time, few of her friends noted any deep sadness or depression on her part. Rather, what some of them saw was an impatience to the point of intolerance with the new postwar world. And some were surprised at her tendency to ignore world affairs and current problems—her disposition to think and talk of the past rather than the future.

To Elizabeth Sergeant, returning from Europe after months of hospitalization resulting from a tragic accident in which the explosion of a mortar had filled her legs with fragments of knife-edged steel, Willa seemed lacking in the sympathy which might have been expected of a friend. Elizabeth, walking painfully in Central Park with the help of two canes, felt that Willa, at her side, was impatient with her; that she wanted her friends whole, able to walk as briskly as she.

But when they were seated at a table in the park and their talk turned inevitably to their writing, Elizabeth hoped she might find herself on the same companionable ground with Willa as of old. It did not work out that way. They talked of writing, but it seemed to Elizabeth that they talked almost entirely of Willa's writing.

As time went on and Elizabeth took up residence in New York only a few blocks from where Willa and Edith lived, the two friends saw each other more frequently than before. Elizabeth discovered then that there were subjects on which she could not communicate with her friend. Willa was no longer in step with the times. They could not discuss the new talents of the twentieth century. Willa would have none of it. She dismissed the free-verse poets with a derogatory word. Sinclair Lewis, she said, was playing at being a sociologist and not seeing as a whole the society of which he wrote. She would take her psychology from Tolstoy as she always had; this new Freud—bah! And Willa's word was final. Elizabeth found her only course was silence. Had Willa changed? Or had she, Elizabeth? Or had they both? At any rate, she found highly distressing her friend's unwillingness to be open-minded, and to give the present a chance.

Again Willa's plans were to take her away from New York when summer came. She was scheduled as a lecturer at the Breadloaf Writers' Conference in Vermont that June of 1922. From there she was going for a visit to the Island of Grand Manan, off the coast of New Brunswick. And finally, back to Jaffrey, New Hampshire, for the autumn months.

It was during 1922 and 1923 that she was working on *A Lost Lady*, which she had begun even before *One of Ours* went out of the Knopf offices to the bookstores.

She had difficulty in getting *A Lost Lady* off to a proper start, which was unusual for her. When she went to Vermont for the Conference, she took two versions of the opening chapters with her to ponder.

Originally, she had laid the story in Colorado, although it was about people she had known in Red Cloud as a child.

She had tried to avoid making this fact obvious by the change in setting, but it hadn't worked that way. Also, she had started to tell the story in the third person. Then she had begun again, placing the story in its true locale, Nebraska, and this time had tried writing it in first person. Now she must come to a decision as to how to proceed.

Before the Conference was over, she had decided to go back to the third-person approach, but to use the Nebraska setting. So at the end of the lecture series, the worshipful, aspiring young writers in attendance were pleased to see the austere novelist, Willa Cather, smile. They were able to take home a warmer picture of her than anticipated, for her smile lighted her severe countenance and made it quite handsome.

Edith Lewis met Willa at the conclusion of the Conference, and they went together to Grand Manan. The island was a new and very different experience. It was only fifteen miles long and seven or eight wide. Most of the people living there were fishermen, clustered in a few small villages around the island, their business and their life to catch herring in their nets and lobster in their traps.

When Willa and Edith arrived, they went to see Sarah Jacobus at Whale Cove. This was not by chance. There had been a definite chain of circumstances that led to the island, Whale Cove, and Miss Jacobus. While doing research at the New York Public Library, Willa had come to know a librarian, Miss Overton, who knew Sarah Jacobus. One day when Willa and Miss Overton were chatting, the matter of the author's need for a quiet place to work came into the conversation. Suddenly Miss Overton thought of the little group of New York women—Barbara Silber, Ethel Manning, Katharine Schwartz, a Mrs. D' Arms, and Sarah Jacobus—all of whom had first disembarked at Grand Manan from a tramp steamer. Sarah Jacobus, she told Willa, had subsequently returned to purchase property at Whale Cove and now operated a small guesthouse there. Miss Overton suggested Grand Manan as an ideal "writing spot," for Ethel Manning had said it was "the most quiet place in the world."

Willa and Edith were enchanted with the Island and taken with its solitude. They would like to stay. Only a few hundred yards from Whale Cove Cottage, Miss Jacobus' home and guesthouse, was another small house which she owned, and in which she rented rooms. Whale Cove Cottage was full when Willa and Edith arrived, so, with some trepidation, the proprietress showed the other accommodations to them. The cottage was a century old, it had no "modern conveniences," and it was drafty and far from tight against wind and chill.

Somewhat to Miss Jacobus' surprise, Willa and Edith took two downstairs rooms. They were charmed with the gray, weathered clapboard of the exterior and with the view of the gray sea from the doorstep. They would take their meals with Miss Jacobus' other guests at Whale Cove Cottage.

Willa and Edith's enchantment with the island did not diminish as the weeks went by; in fact, it increased. They resolved to return another year. With that summer as a beginning, Willa established a pattern which she was to follow for some fifteen years. The summer months she spent on Grand Manan; the autumn months, at Jaffrey.

Other Whale Cove guests and the few tradespeople at North Head, the nearest village, saw little of the "new" ladies, though they saw more of Edith than of Willa. When Edith was alone, they would inquire about her friend. Edith's reply was always the same: Miss Cather was working.

The children on the island sometimes came upon the two women, all of them in a common pursuit, picking the wild flowers which carpeted the meadows. On such occasions, friendly greetings were exchanged. Among themselves, the children called them "the nice ladies."

Islanders of adult vintage, catching a glimpse now and again of the two women climbing high on the cliffs, shook their heads. City folks.

CHAPTER XVI

Willa completed *A Lost Lady* in the spring of 1923. Then she was ready for a vacation. The Hambourgs induced her to come to France to spend some time with them. They had bought a country place a short distance outside Paris, the Ville d'Avray. They prepared a study for her in the hope that her visit might be extended to more than a "vacation."

However, Isabelle found her old friend changed. Although Willa was scarcely old enough to be living in the past, having just turned fifty, she seemed deliberately to be turning against the present. She referred to it as "this tawdry machine age," contrasting it with "the beautiful past." The second generation on her beloved Divide in Nebraska, she said, were not made of the same stuff as their parents. Culture in America had become crass since the War. No one was interested in anything but the Almighty Dollar.

Her friends were not surprised when she did not choose to remain to use the study they had provided her. She did, however, stay long enough to sit for her portrait to be painted by Leon Bakst, a well-known Russian artist who was living in Paris. The Library Board of Omaha, Nebraska, had commissioned the portrait for the city's main library.

Although the artist liked Willa and the two chatted warmly at the sittings, the likeness of her that emerged was disappointing in the extreme. The finished portrait was lifeless, dour, and stiff; nonetheless, it was sent to Omaha and hung.

The sittings over, Willa went to the little town of Aix-les-Bains where she remained for several weeks. As a matter of fact, she grew sufficiently fond of the village to return to it on another occasion.

By autumn she was back at Jaffrey and the Shattuck Inn, where she was becoming something of a tradition.

Lillian Farnsworth, head waitress at the Inn, looked forward to Miss Cather's sojourns there. "She was always very neat," Miss Farnsworth said. "She had what I would call 'a well-scrubbed look.'" She admired Willa's beautiful skin, heavy, dark hair, and deep blue eyes, and the fact that she was always nicely dressed. "She wore coats with fur collars. Most of the time she dressed a little bit mannish—tailored, that is." But there was her fetish about coffee! "She liked it just regular strength, but it had to be *so hot!*"

It was one of the duties of the head waitress to type the daily menus in a little office off the dining room. Willa would pause there and speak to her. Miss Cather, according to the waitress, "had a hearty laugh and a pleasant expression. She wasn't ever cross that I knew of. She didn't mix with the other guests, though, except that she would talk with the old people sometimes after a meal."

The Willa Cather of New York was seen in quite a different light. Strangers who noticed her at the theater or the opera during these years saw a confident, handsome woman, richly dressed, very aloof. They knew her to be a famous novelist. Sometimes at intermission they would approach her, only to be coolly rebuffed.

Even editors like Henry Canby of the then new *Saturday Review* found her extremely frustrating. She refused point-blank to review books for magazines or to be quoted. Nevertheless, as the Canbys lived in the same neighborhood as Willa, Mrs. Canby went one morning to call on Willa and invite her to dinner, not knowing that the morning hours were strictly forbidden to callers. She was much taken aback when, as she stood in the dark entrance of the building, her ring was answered by a woman with an angry face, who peered over the bannister demanding in an annoyed voice, "Who are you and what do you want?" Mrs. Canby stammered that she was Henry Canby's wife, and that she had come to invite Willa to dinner. She was relieved then to see the angry expression turn to a smile. Her invitation was accepted.

Mrs. Canby had invited only one other guest, a young English journalist who was visiting the United States. Willa disliked the young man at sight and made no attempt to disguise the fact. Not only did she make the evening difficult for her hosts; she also told them that she did not wish to be invited again unless their other guests would be people of whom she approved!

Probably all of Willa's acquaintances in the 1920's—with the possible exception of Edith Lewis and a few old friends in Red Cloud, notably Annie Pavelka and Carrie Miner Sherwood—would have agreed that she was difficult at times.

As to Edith's patient role, William Allen White, the famous journalist, once remarked that every Captain must have a First Mate to make the sailing easier, often without the Captain's being aware of it; and that "it takes two to write a book." Though Edith must have had her own private tears, to the world she always insisted that her friend's work must be protected. Over and over again she repeated that Willa did not feel superior or indifferent to the people whom she snubbed. She did what she did as a matter of self-preservation.

But occasionally Willa did grant an interview. Burton Rascoe interviewed her and reported his impressions in both *A Bookman's Daybook* and *Arts and Decorations*. He said that he found her to be very intelligent and a good judge of her own talent; that her standards were high and her sense of values invulnerable. There was nothing false about her. She was capable. He was sure, he said, that she could manage a dairy farm, a law practice, or a magazine with equal effectiveness. He enjoyed her wit and her use of colloquial expressions and forthright Anglo-Saxon words in conversation. He remarked upon her self-confidence, decisiveness, and "stubbornness."

She told him, he said, that musicians and actors fascinated her because they took her into a world of illusion, that their ability to furnish an escape was their chief charm.

Willa's ideas in regard to artistic writing had now taken definite shape. In an essay entitled "The Novel Demeuble," she expressed the opinion that "cataloging," and the use of excessive detail have no place in the artistic novel. "The novel, for a long while, has been over-furnished," she said.

A Lost Lady showed ample evidence of the application of her theory. Almost all of the critics met the book with acclaim for its economy of style.

It was the story of Marian Forrester, a character based on Mrs. Silas Garber whom the author said was "a woman I loved very much in my childhood." It was a masterful portrait of the lady.

Marian was the young wife of a railroad contractor much older than she, who had built hundreds of miles of road for the Burlington in the Midwest. The Forresters had a very fine home in the small town of "Sweet Water," Nebraska, where railroad dignitaries were frequently entertained.

Marian Forrester possessed qualities which charmed all who came. She was "a very special kind of person"—exciting, bewitching, lovely. Yet even before the accident which incapacitated her husband, she was having an affair with a younger man from Denver.

Then came the financial crash, in which the Forresters lost heavily. As a result, their way of life was vastly altered. "Captain" Forrester had a stroke and died, but he had kept his dignity to the end—a symbol of the great years of "the building of the West." His wife, however, refused to give in gracefully after the passing of the splendid pioneer period of which he had made her a part.

Following her husband's death, Marian took up with an unscrupulous, uncouth young lawyer, Ivy Peters. She entertained the "boys" of the town, men much younger than she and completely lacking her cultural background. She was "a lost lady."

A mere postscript ended the story: Marian had eventually left Sweet Water for California, there met and married a "rich, cranky" old man and lived out her last years with him in Buenos Aires.

It was a short book. The characterization was masterfully done in sharp, sure strokes. And with Marian Forrester's story, smoothly integrated, went the symbolization of the proud strength of the era when the West was won; of the decadence in the period which followed. *A Lost Lady* was one of Willa Cather's best books; by many, it has been considered her finest.

It also marked the halfway point in her novel output. It was her sixth. Six more were to follow.

CHAPTER XVII

Book number seven was *The Professor's House.* In it some discerned a new theme for Willa Cather—religion. This theme was to become even more prominent in two of her very fine future books, notably in *Death Comes for the Archbishop* and, to a lesser degree, in *Shadows on the Rock.*

Yet none of Willa's friends ever mentioned hearing her discuss religion, except to say that she felt faith was hard to come by. It was the feeling of her first and authorized biographer, E. K. Brown, that art had been her god previously; that at this time art and religion seemed to fuse into one for her.

There were other indications of her new interest in religion. In December, 1922, with her parents, she had joined the Episcopal Church in Red Cloud. Willa had grown up in the Baptist Church, attending with her family as a matter of course. But now, at fifty, she made a deliberate choice of a creed which she felt would be more rewarding to her. Both the form of the Episcopal Church, with its emphasis on ritual and music, and the tie with the past which it represented were in line with her interests.

She had also written an essay regarding Joseph Mann's *Joseph and His Brethern.* In this she had expressed her appreciation of his treatment of Man's struggle to find his relation to the Universe. The essay showed, too, her familiarity with the Bible. Its stories and characters were all meaningful to her as a part of the tapestry of the past, of Western civilization's religious heritage from the Jews.

When *The Professor's House* appeared in 1925, it was met with criticism which ran the scale of the Professor's own poor-to-excellent grading system. It is still a controversial book.

Reading it is like finding a pearl in an oyster. In the gray, dreary story of Professor Godfrey St. Peter is embedded the vivid, polished tale of Tom Outland. Ironically, the setting for the aging Professor's story was the then-contemporary period of post World War I; the setting for Young Outland's, an ancient Cliff Dwellers' village, centuries old.

Professor St. Peter and his wife, when the story opened, had just moved from an old rented house, where they had long lived, to a newly built home of their own. The money for the new house was prize money awarded the Professor for a fine, creative series of historical books he had written—his life's work. The Professor did not really want the new house. He compromised by retaining his cramped, musty study on the third floor of the old house, paying rent on the whole property in order to do so.

Tom Outland had been a student of the Professor's. While in college, he had discovered a gas which was to become important in the development of aviation. But he was called to the front in France and was killed. In his will, he had left everything to one of the Professor's daughters, Rosamond. She had since married, and her husband had seen and taken advantage of the commercial possibilities of Outland's patent. As a result, the couple became wealthy almost overnight.

One outcome of this was that all of the Professor's family spent a summer in Europe while he, of his own volition, remained at home. In their absence he lived in the old house. One night he was nearly asphixiated and would have been had not the maid, Augusta, found and saved him. Prior to this time, he had been increasingly possessed by a weariness of life. He felt there was nothing left in it for him, and thought he could not bear to return to the new house when his family came home. But after his close brush with death and his rescue by Augusta—who represented religion in the book—he felt that he could go on because of Augusta and the people and ideas she represented.

The Tom Outland story, which seemed almost an oversight in the telling, was brought into the novel when the young man himself told it to Professor St. Peter. It was the tale of the meeting and friendship of Tom and Rapp, of their being hired as cowboys in New Mexico, and of their discovery of "Cliff City," a long-lost Indian Pueblo. After they had carefully preserved their findings and husbanded their meager savings, Tom made a trip to Washington, D.C., to try to interest the government. But he got only a series of runarounds, and the result was tremendous disappointment. Worse yet, when Tom returned to the mesa, he found that Rapp had sold the Indian artifacts for four thousand dollars and they had been removed. This was not at all what Tom had envisioned for them. He had hoped to have an ancient civilization revived through scholarly study by archeologists. The differences of the men as to what was and was not precious in life caused Rapp to leave and brought an end to their friendship.

Disagreement over the effectiveness of this book has stemmed largely from different views of the inclusion of the Tom Outland story. Some critics felt that there were two separate stories in the book, and that they did not belong under one cover. Others thought the novel had a fine subtle unity, that the two stories were carefully wrought and each added to the dimension of the other.

The two divergent opinions in regard to the book seem basically to have resulted from its being read on two different levels. Those who read it on the literal level only, thought it a slender tale and could see no point in the story-within-a-story, which they felt had little bearing on the plot. Those who read it on a symbolic level felt that Willa Cather's use of houses produced a unity into which the "intruding" story fit nicely.

Willa herself attempted to explain the Tom Outland story by saying she was trying to get the kind of effect achieved by the old Dutch masters who painted interiors with a window which brought in the sun and light and movement of the outside world. In his book, *Pioneers and Caretakers*, Louis Auchincloss later said, "One may be struck by this idea and still doubt that she brought it off."

Another critic, Alfred Kazin, has referred to *The Professor's House* as the most underrated of Willa Cather's novels. He believes it ranks high in literary maturity.

The fact remains that most readers cannot be sympathetic with the disgruntled, middle-aged man who fills the pages of three-fourths of the book. There was no doubt now that Willa was showing her own age and her own disgruntlement with the postwar world.

In the same year as the release of *The Professor's House*, 1925, Willa and Edith moved into their first "house"—a cottage of their own on Grand Manan. After a couple of seasons of rented quarters on the island, they had decided to have a cottage of their own built, not far from that of Miss Jacobus. In the summer of 1925, it was ready for them.

From that time on, Willa spent more time than usual in virtual isolation. With several months in the island cottage and several at Jaffrey, she was less and less available to friends and acquaintances in New York.

Then, too, there were other trips to the Southwest. The first of these occurred as soon as Willa had *The Professor's House* off her hands. And it was on this occasion that she came face to face with the material that inspired her novel, *Death Comes for the Archbishop*, though she was to write and publish another short book before it.

Edith again accompanied Willa, and they headquartered in Santa Fe.

There was a sizable library in the La Fonda Hotel where they stayed, and Willa was soon engrossed in reading. One night she read until nearly dawn. The volume with which she was so fascinated was *The Life of the Right Reverend Joseph P. Machebeuf*. Written by Father W. J. Howlett and privately printed, it told the life story of Father Machebeuf, a pioneer priest in New Mexico who eventually became the first Bishop of Denver. It was Willa's "find" of the summer. In it she had discovered the theme for *Death Comes for the Archbishop*.

While in Santa Fe, Willa received an invitation to visit the Luhan Ranch near Taos, some seventy-five miles distant. The invitation came from Mabel Dodge Luhan, a wealthy patroness of the arts and white wife of Tony Luhan, a remarkable Taos Indian. She asked Willa to come to them for an extended visit. Willa refused, saying she did not "visit." Mabel assured her that she and Edith would have a house to themselves, and that Willa's working hours would not be disturbed. At last, Willa agreed to go to the ranch for two or three days.

As Mabel had promised, her guest was not disturbed, and the two or three days stretched into three weeks. In the long afternoons after Willa had laid her work aside, Tony would drive her and Edith about the countryside. He enjoyed showing "his" country to these two women, for they responded to its beauty, liked its sagebrush and sunflowers, and were genuinely interested in the remote villages to which he took them. He enjoyed the questions Willa asked. They were not "tourist" questions; they indicated a sincere desire to learn.

After dinner in the evening, they all sat in the Big House. It was colorful with cages of brilliant parrots. Rich with art treasures. Tony was impressive in his long braids and beautiful blanket. Silent, he usually played solitaire. The others conversed. Mabel tried in vain to interest Willa in the Pueblo Indians as a tribal people, and in her own political struggle to save their lands and traditions.

To Mabel, Willa's lack of interest was an enigma, since her frequent visits to the Southwest indicated an interest in the area. Surely she must be thinking of writing a book about it. And what was the country without its Pueblo Indians?

Willa, however, was primarily concerned with the French

priests of the early days; she was interested more in those who had ministered to the Indians than she was in the Indians. Also, the Willa Cather who could always espouse the causes of individuals but not of groups was again showing her colors.

But even though Mabel found this one matter frustrating and disappointing, she did not discount Willa's contribution to literature. At the close of the visit, she invited Willa to return the following summer, and this Willa did.

CHAPTER XVIII

Meanwhile, a short novel, *My Mortal Enemy*, had appeared. Like *A Lost Lady*, it was a portrait. But in the new book, Willa applied even more astringently than before the principle she had propounded: "How wonderful it would be if we could throw all the furniture out of the window and leave the room as bare as the stage of a Greek theatre . . . leave the scene bare for the play of emotions. . . ."

The stage was indeed uncluttered in *My Mortal Enemy*. She had thrown out everything but the bare set. The story was so short that there was some question about its being a novel; yet Alfred Knopf agreed to publish it in book form, alone, as Willa wished it to appear.

It was the story of Myra Henshaw, ward of a wealthy uncle, who as a girl had run away to marry her lover not of her faith, thereby cutting herself out of her uncle's estate. For a time the young couple prospered, but eventually they fell on evil days. Oswald, the husband, lost his money, and Myra lost her health.

Myra became convinced that she had made a mistake in giving up money for love. In the last part of the book, she turned on her husband ferociously, blaming him for their lack of money, for her break with the Church, for all their ills. In the end, she died alone on a headland by the sea. Shortly before her death, she said, in her husband's presence, "Why must I die like this, alone with my mortal enemy?"

Some readers have thought Myra referred to her husband as her "mortal enemy." Others have believed she referred to herself—to the person she became through the determined exercise of her own will.

Whichever the interpretation, it was a bitter book. Myra Henshaw as protagonist was surely the most unlikable character Willa Cather ever portrayed. Now Willa's feeling that in the 1920's "the world broke in two" was darkening her fiction.

Her friends found her old fount of good talk flowing less often and less freely. As for acquaintances, she simply had no words at all; they would have been a waste of time and energy. Willa took herself and her writing very seriously. She was working steadily—and, it seemed, happily—on her story of the Archbishop.

In the summer of 1926, she returned to the Southwest to verify certain facts and gather further material for the book. Edith again accompanied her. They headquartered in Santa Fe as before. However, a side trip to Acoma to visit a pueblo afforded an unexpected but rewarding experience. En route, they were forced to spend a week in a dilapidated little hotel in the village of Laguna.

This village was as close as they could get to Acoma by train. Here Willa had planned to hire a car to take them the remaining thirty miles. However, a violent rainstorm descended upon the town the night of their arrival and for days deluged the area. The road to Acoma was impassable for a week.

Despite the sorry accommodations—the worst they had ever had anywhere—the enforced stay was far from the intellectual sludge expected. It was, instead, a literary spring. Here, among the laconic Laguna Indians, Willa absorbed some of her best material for the novel on which she was working.

When she left the Southwest that summer, she went again to New Hampshire. But instead of returning to the Shattuck Inn in Jaffrey, she went to the MacDowell Colony at Peterborough, only a few miles distant.

The MacDowell Colony had been founded in 1901 by

the widow of Edward MacDowell, the composer, as a memorial to her husband. It was a beautiful four-hundred-acre retreat for artists in all fields. It embodied a modified style of communal living. Each artist had his own studio in which to work. These were small individual cabins scattered invitingly among the pine woods far enough apart so that one, working, could feel quite alone. This feature of the Colony appealed strongly to Willa.

Mrs. MacDowell, the major domo of the Colony, welcomed Willa Cather with enthusiasm, but her enthusiasm soon waned as she discovered that Willa would make no concessions to community living. Mrs. MacDowell was not only the "Autocrat of the Breakfast Table," she was also the Autocrat of the Dinner Table, the Autocrat of the Evening Hours—the Autocrat, in fact of HER Colony. She did not like the fact that Willa was usually not where she was supposed to be, *when* she was supposed to be there. Nor did she like the fact that Willa, though always respectful, did not pay court to her as her other guests did. But respect or no, Willa was aloof, and Mrs. MacDowell sensed disapproval more often than approval in her unsmiling face.

The Colony's daily chronology, developed by Mrs. MacDowell, was as follows: Breakfast (dining room) 7:30 A.M. (announced by the clang-clang of a raucous bell); cold basket lunch, served in the cabins (actually, left on the doorsteps) at noon; dinner, communal style, in the dining room at 6:30 P.M.; and then an evening of talk and music and even games, with Marian MacDowell, herself, presiding.

At breakfast, Mrs. MacDowell's eagle eye did not have to search for Willa Cather; she knew her "problem child" would be there, eating heartily and demanding that her coffee be hotter than hot, eating silently, her eyes on her plate, dispatching the food in businesslike fashion. She would be one of the first to excuse herself and depart briskly and determinedly for her workshop. This was the time of day when Marian MacDowell liked Willa Cather best.

But later in the day, probably on the very stroke of

twelve, when Mrs. MacDowell was delivering lunches, driving from studio to studio in her buggy, she might see Willa striding off in the direction of the Village, and this did not please the "Autocrat." Her food was good enough for her other guests! Yet Willa was obviously going into town to eat at an inn—leaving her work when there were still four or five fine daylight hours for writing. And at times there was someone else with her. Marian MacDowell's annoyance was then even greater. Not only was Willa not fitting into the pattern; she was leading others astray and disrupting the well-planned order of the Colony.

Willa was used to doing her work in the morning hours, then leaving it until the following morning, when she would return to it fresh and eager. She was used to a hearty, hot meal at noon, after her day's work was finished, and since such was not furnished at MacDowell, she simply went where she could get it.

Evenings were even worse. When the guests assembled in the library after dinner, Willa was invariably absent. Mrs. MacDowell would send someone to look for her with the message that her hostess wished to see her. More often than not, the messenger returned without having found the recalcitrant one; or, having found her, with the reply that Willa sent her regrets—but she was reading a book which she wished to finish or had letters to write.

Years later, Mrs. MacDowell said that when Willa Cather was in residence at the Colony, she was continually escaping pursuit.

The other guests—with the exception of a few whom Willa liked and to whom she was, therefore, civil—openly disapproved of her insistence on her right to solitude. In the old red farmhouse known as "The Eaves," where the women had their sleeping quarters, one or another of the women guests would invade Willa's privacy as soon as the evening's festivities had broken up (which was early, for Mrs. MacDowell believed in an early bedtime). They all knew Willa would not respond with warmth to a call, and they were particularly prone to make these forays if they felt she had been "high and mighty" at dinner that evening.

At Shattuck Inn, there were rumors that Willa Cather was finding it "too cold" at the Colony. They thought she meant the weather!

CHAPTER XIX

The year 1927 brought Willa deep satisfaction due to the happy reception of *Death Comes for the Archbishop*. With the publication of this book, the critics and the public alike were laudatory.

The critics were beginning to note that Willa Cather was no "formula writer," that for each story she told she chose the form best fitted to it. In *Death Comes for the Archbishop*, she used the form of legend, something she had wanted to try all her life. Certainly this form was admirably suited to the material.

The book was comprised of the intermingled life stories of two Catholic priests in the Southwest: Father Vaillant and Father Latour. Together, the two had come to America directly from their seminary training in France. First located in Canada, they were, at the opening of the book, en route to a newly formed bishopric in New Mexico. Of a vast, sprawling area of mountains and desert, Father Latour had been named Bishop.

Father Latour was the idealist and the scholar; Father Vaillant, the realist and the man of the people. The two ministered to Mexicans, Indians, and whites for many years. Near the close of their lives, they were separated, for Father Vaillant had been sent to Colorado as spiritual adviser to the miners, and was thereafter made the first Bishop of Denver.

The very fine relationship between the two priests, between each of them and the peoples of the region, and the appreciation of both men for all that made up the Southwest constituted the fabric of this book.

The story was told with such sincerity that countless people who read it, even among the Catholic clergy, thought that Willa was a Catholic.

In this novel she had returned to the simple, unaffected narrative of human life that she had used in *My Antonia*. She had fused setting and characters to perfection. She had used a quiet style that was beautifully appropriate. She had told each story and legend within the book so that it was complete in itself, yet made each progressively a part of the whole. And above all, her use of language and her imagery made the New Mexican landscape glow with color and live in beauty.

Death Comes for the Archbishop has won a permanent place in American letters, and is considered one of the best books written in the first half of the century.

There was no question as to whether or not Willa would return to the MacDowell Colony in the autumn of 1927. No one expected her to give the "experiment" a second try. However, she was expected at the Shattuck Inn in Jaffrey again that fall. The usual preparations were made for her arrival, and mail began streaming in for her.

When she arrived, the Shattucks, their daughter, and the employees all noticed that Willa was in a particularly mellow mood. The daily influx of mail obviously pleased her, and after reading a large bundle of it, she was often glowing and, for her, quite expansive.

To her friend Lillian Farnsworth, the head waitress, she mentioned that her heavy but rewarding mail was largely in response to *Death Comes for the Archbishop*. Many of her letters, she said, were from the clergy, all of whom seemed pleased with the book. It gave her great satisfaction, she explained, for this was a "different" kind of book from any she had written before. She had had doubts as to how it would be received.

Edith Lewis had not yet come to Jaffrey that season, and Willa said she was getting very anxious for her friend to arrive so that, among other things, she could help answer the letters.

In the meantime, she started writing something new. She was never one "to let the grass grow under her feet." Most mornings the kitchen staff was asked to have a good luncheon packed for her by the time she finished breakfast. A cab would then come for her, collect her, her lunch, her camp chair, and her writing materials, and she would not be seen again until afternoon. She took the cab to Gap Mountain, about four miles from the Inn. "I don't know how far she went up the mountain after the cab driver left her," Lillian Farnsworth said, "but she was a good walker."

Eventually Edith did arrive. According to Lillian Farnsworth, "She was very, very nice." But no one saw much of her, as she was busy typing most of the time.

Apparently happier than for some years past, Willa returned to New York at the end of autumn. But the interlude was to be brief.

She went to Red Cloud for Christmas and New Year's, and while she was there, her father had an attack of angina, his first. However, he rallied, and when his improvement seemed steady, Willa left for the East to pick up her work once more. She did not see her father again. In March, he had another attack and death came quickly.

Immediately, Willa set out on the long train trip which she had made so often from New York to Red Cloud. When the funeral was over, it was decided in family conclave that Mrs. Cather needed a rest and a change. Douglass was then living in California, and he suggested that she return home with him. Mrs. Cather, not her usual decisive self, was willing to do whatever her children thought best.

So the house in Red Cloud was closed. But Willa had no home in New York to which to return. Number Five Bank Street, which had been a sanctuary for her for fifteen years, was a sanctuary no more. She and Edith had been forced to move in the fall because the building was to be torn down. They had gone to the Grosvenor Hotel temporarily, and few personal possessions were unpacked. Furniture and trunks were put into storage.

The hotel accommodations were cramped and gloomy, but eventually summer came to lift Willa's spirits with the prospect of Grand Manan.

The two women decided to take a different route to the island this time, going by way of Quebec. It was a fortunate decision. This French city on the North American Continent caught hold of Willa's imagination, excited and pleased her. She had always been fond of France, its culture and traditions. Here, looking down from the windows of the Frontenac Hotel on the city below, she saw Norman architecture. Roaming the streets, she discovered French convents, heard the French language spoken. Her senses were stirred. Her creative impulses quickened. A story of Old Quebec, the city built on a rock! Willa's mind was busy as she and Edith continued their journey to Grand Manan.

As their boat approached the island, the red-topped, white-bodied Whistle Lighthouse beckoned. This first view of the island was particularly enchanting to Willa because Whale Cove and the cottage were on Whistle Road. At long last, she had the feeling that she was coming home.

The cottage on Grand Manan was the only house Willa and Edith ever owned. (The deed was in the name of Edith Lewis, but the cottage was regarded as Willa's, or "theirs.") Their good caretakers, the Beals, had, as usual, made all ready for their arrival. The cottage had been scrubbed. There was wood in the woodbox and ice in the little wooden refrigerator. Chimneys had been cleaned. Furniture uncovered. Rugs swept and aired. Pillows plumped. Wicks of the kerosene lamps trimmed. Linens freshly stacked. Silver polished. Lawn cut. Flower beds hoed. There were staples in the cupboard.

In Willa's workroom in the loft, the newly oiled Oliver typewriter stood ready on the small writing table which had been made short-legged to accommodate the limbs of the user.

Other Grand Mananites had also been alerted to the homecoming—the brothers Gilmore, Claude and Ray, who ran a taxi service; and Miss Jacobus and her staff at Whale Cove where Willa and Edith took their meals.

One of the Gilmores always met the boat to take the two women from port to cottage. From the time of Willa's arrival, they would have certain regular duties: to take one or the other or both of the women to town once a week to do their marketing; to take Willa once during the summer to an Anglican tea; to take the two to North Head for the spectacular view of rock cliffs and ocean spray.

Three times each day during the months of their stay on the island, Willa and Edith walked from their cottage to Whale Cove Inn. Even for breakfast, they came in hats and white cotton gloves—"as though they were on Fifth Avenue," one amused, sophisticated guest remarked. They looked neither to right nor left, she said, as they went through the communal room to the dining room and their table in an alcove.

Breakfast was the only meal for which there was a choice of menu. Each morning Willa ordered four slices of underdone bacon, "the way the English do it," she said; toast, and Sanka. Early in the season she brought her own pot for the Sanka.

It was a good, productive summer for Willa.

After returning to New York and the Grosvenor, she felt impelled to visit Quebec again. She made the trip at Thanksgiving, thus getting to see her enchanted city under the magic of snow. She was hard at work on the book about it, to be called *Shadows on the Rock*.

A month later, however, she received word from her brother Douglass in California that their mother had suffered a cerebral hemmorhage. Willa left immediately for the West Coast to help make arrangements for her mother's care.

She and Douglass searched diligently for a satisfactory place for Mrs. Cather. They found a sanatorium in Pasadena which seemed best. Here they could secure a private cottage for her, with a nurse in constant attendance. Willa was able to rent a separate cottage for herself on the sanatorium grounds. That way she could be with her mother as much as was wise. But her work on the book which French Quebec had inspired could not be continued under these circumstances. However, she could read. So she immersed herself in the land and times of the early settlement on "The Rock" during the period of Count Frontenac's governorship. She studied copious histories, memoirs, and letters relating to seventeenth-century Quebec.

Willa's empathy with her mother in those days was almost complete. She felt great compassion for her, identifying with this proud, independent woman who was paralyzed and could scarcely speak, though still mentally alert. The experience was a great emotional drain upon Willa.

When she returned to New York, her friends saw that her mother's illness had saddened her perhaps even more than her father's death. Yet she was able to get back to the composition of the novel.

Intermittently, she and Edith looked for another apartment, but Willa's heart did not seem to be in the search. Elizabeth Sergeant, having tea with her, realized that at least part of the problem was that Willa simply didn't know what she wanted to do. She thought of New York as having become a maze of money-seekers, everyone rushing madly to get nowhere. Restrictions hemmed one in. People! People! Always bothering one. Perhaps a home in the country would be best, she said tentatively; but Edith wanted to continue to work in the city. And living in the country would present new problems.

Elizabeth had learned, over the years, that Willa never faced change easily. Now the possibility of a whole new way of living obviously upset her. She thought she didn't want to stay in New York, yet she couldn't imagine going elsewhere. She was a depressed, sad, deeply troubled, aging woman, though she still lacked five years of being sixty.

Besides warring with herself over a place to live, she was also warring with herself over the age-old fact of life and death. At the moment, she seemed unable to cope with her problems. Yet Elizabeth was startled when Willa asked her if she thought psychoanalysis might help. She did not think Willa a likely subject for the psychiatrist's couch. She answered that a psychiatrist had advised her, Elizabeth, against attempting to write and be psychoanalyzed at the same time. She left the Grosvenor that afternoon saddened by the uncertainties which were torturing her friend.

The next year brought no solution to Willa's personal problems. Yet she continued to work steadily on *Shadows on the Rock*. She went again to the West Coast to spend time with her mother, who was failing.

That winter she returned once more to Quebec. Then she decided she must go to France.

Reports from California were no better and no worse. But she wanted to spend some time with her mother again before going abroad. So—still in the years when one traveled by train rather than by plane—she once more made the long, tiring journey from coast to coast.

At long last, in May of 1930, friends saw Willa and Edith off for France. Would the book in process profit from the journey? Written under the shadow of Willa's depression, could it possibly equal her splendid story of Father Vaillant and Father Latour?

CHAPTER XX

Two very special things happened to Willa in France that summer of 1930.

First, however, there were old friends, and there was business. She visited Jan and Isabelle Hambourg, finding to her sorrow that Isabelle was not at all well.

But most of her time she spent in visiting the pre-Quebec environs of Count Frontenac, who was a basic character in the book on which she was working. She also rounded out her research in libraries and museums, running down facts she had not been able to verify before.

When these matters were disposed of, she and Edith traveled to the south of France on a real vacation. Their ultimate destination was Aix-les-Bains, a spot Willa had particularly enjoyed on previous visits. Hence she was in an unusually mellow mood as they journeyed toward the town. Unfortunately, when they arrived, it was to find that the little hotel where she had stayed before had been torn down. Even here, the things of character must be swept ruthlessly away by the new broom of "progress"! Willa turned bitter and gloomy again.

The two checked in at a beautiful hotel, Le Splendide, which lived up to its name in every way. The furnishings were plush, balconies were plentiful, tubbed orange trees on the terrace bloomed with lights in the evening, an orchestra played during the dinner hour, the guest list was fabulous. Luxury hotels were anathema to Willa. She paced her room like a caged animal, grumbled and growled like one, and refused to settle down in this atmosphere. To stay there would ruin her visit in her beloved Aix-les-Bains.

She went to the English bank to change some money, and while there, spiritedly voiced her unhappiness over the splendor with which Le Splendide was smothering her. Fortunately, the clerk who waited on her found it amusing that anyone would be discontented with Le Splendide. He suggested Le Grand Hotel d'Aix, an old hotel in the downtown area, and to this the two women hastily moved. However, no one could have foreseen how fortunate this move was to be.

An elderly Frenchwoman of obvious distinction and character was staying at the hotel. Willa and Edith noticed her first in the dining room. Willa was intrigued by her as she often was with old people. She admired the woman's fine head, held so erectly, and the fact that even though the lady was lame, she ignored the handicap, walked with brisk, quick steps.

The lady in question, who spent several months in the hotel each year, was also attracted by the two new guests. It had not taken her long to discover that the larger woman, with the fine blue eyes, was an American novelist. She might be an interesting person to know. Certainly she was not a typical American tourist.

One evening the Frenchwoman was in the lounge at the same time as Willa, who was writing letters. The woman pulled her shawl about her, so Willa got up and closed the window. The Frenchwoman thanked her, then started a conversation in English: Had the American been here before? . . . Oh, yes, and had returned because she liked it so much; Aix-les-Bains seemed a place which changed less than most. Willa smiled as she saw the other's eyes light up at her comment.

The Frenchwoman turned to one of her own chief reasons for coming, the concerts. She would see if this, too, was a point of contact. She was disappointed when Willa said she had not seen *Tristan and Iseult* the evening before at the Grand-Cercle because it had been so hot. But, undaunted, the old lady pursued the subject: Was the American going to the concert the next afternoon? It would be very good, and it was no hotter at Le Grand-Cercle than any place else. This time she received an affirmative reply.

Willa was addressing her in "primer prose," and this she did not appreciate. So she explained that she understood English perfectly and that she had spoken it well at one time. If she did not speak it fluently now, she said, it was because she had had little opportunity to use the language recently.

Willa went to the concert the next afternoon, but she thought the heat unbearable. That evening she asked the Frenchwoman's advice about hotels in the mountains of Haute-Savoie, explaining that she and her friend had decided to escape from the heat.

Willa and Edith left and were gone for a couple of weeks. When they returned to Le Grand Hotel, the Frenchwoman was still there. Willa thanked her for her suggestions regarding hotels in the mountains, saying they had enjoyed their stay greatly.

Still, there had been no introductions between Willa and this woman. They sat down together in the lounge and began conversing. The Frenchwoman remarked that she had known Turgenev, the Russian author. Turgenev, she explained, had been a great friend of her uncle, and she had been brought up in her uncle's home. Once when Turgenev visited there, she had been doing a translation of *Faust*, just for her own enjoyment. He had gone over her translation and made corrections.

Willa, smiling and leaning forward, was a most attentive audience. So the Frenchwoman continued: Her mother had died when she was born, and she had been raised by her uncle.

"My uncle was a man of letters," she said. "He was Gustave Flaubert. Perhaps you know——"

Willa did not reply in words. She bent toward Madame Grout, took one of her hands, and kissed it.

The woman could not possibly have known how much

her revelation would mean to Willa. This was Flaubert's niece Caroline! The "Caro" of his letters! Willa Cather had actually met Madame Grout, famed niece of her revered Flaubert, whom she had read with the Seibels in Pittsburgh, whose works she admired so greatly!

One morning Willa told Madame Grout that she must leave that very day because of the illness of a dear friend in Paris. Madame Grout invited Willa to return to the South of France and visit her at her home, the Villa Tanit, in Antibes, before returning to America. She was very disappointed when Willa said she feared this would have to wait until another summer. Madame was further disappointed, and a little hurt, when she offered to send Willa some artifact of her uncle's or one of his letters, only to be refused again. "Souvenirs" meant little to her, Willa said.

Madame Grout and Willa Cather were never to see each other again. The Frenchwoman died the following February.

Willa's sudden call back to Paris was from Jan Hambourg, who wired that his wife's condition had worsened. However, after Willa and Edith had been in Paris a short time, Isabelle improved somewhat, and Jan offered to take the guests to a concert. As a result, another meeting, most fortunate for Willa, occurred that summer.

Jan had become interested in a young violinist from the States, "a child prodigy" by the name of Yehudi Menuhin, who was appearing in Paris. It was to hear this artist that he took Willa and Edith. They were enthralled with his performance.

At the conclusion of the concert, Jan offered to take them to the young virtuoso's dressing room to meet him. With him was his mother, who was astute and an excellent judge of character. She was immediately interested in Willa, and invited her to call at the Menuhin apartment in Paris.

Willa went and was accepted by the entire Menuhin family. So began the Menuhin-Cather friendship which soon gave the Menuhin children the privilege of calling her

"Aunt Willa." Many years later, Yehudi Menuhin said, "It was as if each one of us had a private wire to Aunt Willa. She was not just a friend of the family. She was a friend of each one of us as an individual."

There were the two little girls, Hepzibah and Yaltah, expected to practice the piano with almost as much dedication as Yehudi was expected to practice the violin. They greeted their caller with European formality but with little smiles of genuine welcome. This guest did not talk down to them nor seem to be uneasy with them because they were children. They talked this over afterward with Yehudi and all three agreed that they liked this new friend. Their mother also liked her. They would see each other again when they were all back in New York.

However, Willa did not return to New York for some time. She had booked passage home on the Empress Line, which went by way of Quebec. Originally she had intended to disembark at Boston and go from there to Jaffrey to write. But when the Empress docked at Quebec, with the October woods outlining the St. Lawrence, the city on the rock beckoned too strongly for her to resist. She stopped off there once more.

CHAPTER XXI

When Willa did arrive in Jaffrey, somewhat later than her luggage and later than she had been expected, her friends and acquaintances soon discovered that they were to see very little of her during her stay that autumn. She was engrossed in her writing. *Shadows on the Rock* was going well, and she was in good spirits.

She did, however, occasionally sit down to chat with other guests in the evening. Among these were Alice and Neilson Edwards. Later Mrs. Edwards recalled how intently Willa had listened to Neilson tell about his hunting trips. She seemed able, without effort, to draw him out to talk of the animals and the woods and his experiences. It was Alice Edwards' feeling that these things to which Willa listened with such interest were usually things she could make use of in her books.

She liked the authoress, however, considered her a wonderful person, and was glad that she and her husband were among "the favored ones." She recalled having made a comment to Willa on the good looks of a young woman who was staying at the Inn. Willa's reply had been typical: "Good looking? With that mean little mouth?"

When the Shattucks and Austermanns (Eleanor Shattuck had married George Austermann.) saw Willa off for New York after her two months' stay with them that autumn, they were bidding farewell "until next year," not just to a guest but to a friend. She had been coming to the Shattuck for thirteen years and was to continue until she had rounded out two decades. The fact that in those years her fame as a novelist had grown steadily was not of first importance to them. She was most of all a friend who loved Mt. Monadnock better than the Alps or the Rockies, a friend who had needed their protection, had received it, and had appreciated it.

Back in the gloom of the Grosvenor, Willa saw few people, for she was reaching the end of *Shadows on the Rock,* writing steadily, rapidly, and surely. She finished it a few days after Christmas.

Alfred Knopf had long since learned that if he were to keep one of his most productive and successful novelists happy and producing, he must protect her from the pressures and interruptions which are the usual accouterments of fame. This he did, sheltering Willa in New York much as the Shattucks did in Jaffrey. He and his wife always remembered Willa on her birthday and at Christmas, made occasional social calls on her, and thought of her as a friend. But they intruded on her privacy very little. They thought of her as "dear" in the best sense of the word, and the gifts they sent her were in keeping. A pair of Venetian glass bottles for salad oil and vinegar were typical.

When the manuscript of *Shadows on the Rock* was in Knopf's hands, two factors persuaded Willa to go West again. One was an invitation from the University of California to accept an honorary doctoral degree. The other was a letter from Douglass in California, saying their mother was growing continually weaker.

Those closest to Willa realized that her mother's long illness was both a physical and spiritual drain on the daughter. Edith was concerned to hear that, after reaching Pasadena, Willa had spent considerable time in bed with a bad case of bronchitis, an ailment which attacked her in times of stress or exhaustion.

One of the "slips" that can occur in the script of the best of authors, came very near to reaching print in *Shadows on the Rock.* The book had been set up in type, and Willa had read and approved both galley and page proofs before the error was discovered. When she was leaving for California, she asked Edith to read foundry proofs for her—the last look before the actual run of a book.

Edith was amazed while reading them to receive a telegram from Willa saying that throughout the entire book the term "Archbishop," used as a title before "Laval" and "de Saint-Vallier" was to be changed to read "Bishop." A Catholic friend in San Francisco had caught the error.

When *Shadows on the Rock* came out, it was generally well received and reviews were favorable. This did not, however, bring the usual lift to Willa's spirits. She seemed to be settling into a lethargic sadness, regardless of critical acclaim.

Laid in Quebec in the seventeenth century, *Shadows on the Rock* was basically a father-daughter book. It made those who knew Willa well think the relationship it portrayed was fashioned after her own relationship with her father. It was loving, understanding, and rewarding. The father of the story was a French apothecary, Euclide Auclair. He had come to Quebec in the service of Count de Frontenac when the Count was made Governor of the Colony. Auclair's daughter Cecile had been trained well by her mother in the long months of illness which preceded the mother's death. Cecile looked after the house and her father in an adult and sensitive manner and was happy in the service. She loved "The Rock" which was Quebec.

When it looked as though Count de Frontenac would return to France, taking the Auclairs with him, Cecile was very unhappy. However, the old Count died, and Cecile and her father remained in Quebec. Eventually, Cecile married there and established her own home and family.

Something of a sub-plot also ran through the book in the story of the "old" Bishop, Father Laval and the "new," Monseigneur de Saint-Vallier. Between these two characters, there was effective contrast. Through it Willa showed her preference for the values represented by Father Laval.

The book had a quiet, serene tone very fitting for the story. For life in this little colony perched high on a great rock was, though rigorous, quiet and unexciting. There was not a great deal of conflict in the story. It seemed a long lyric prose poem, sincere, genuine, and charming.

There was considerable use of symbolism—the concentrated symbol of the Rock, the symbolic use of the seasons. And once again, as in the early Nebraska novels and *Death Comes for the Archbishop,* Willa showed her admiration for the pioneer spirit.

Some reviewers felt the book lacked vitality and indicated a diminution of the author's power. Yet she received the French award, the *Prix Femina Américaine,* for the novel.

Willa's friends did note at this time, however, a diminishing of her physical vigor which accompanied her growing despondency. Her mother's long-anticipated death occurred in the summer of 1931, and with it Willa's withdrawal became even greater. It saddened those who were close to her to see that the vitality which had seemed her central force appeared to be drying up. It saddened them even more because she was not yet sixty.

CHAPTER XXII

The Christmas after her mother's death, Willa returned to Red Cloud for the last time. In the fall, Lizzie Huffman, who had been a housekeeper of the elder Cathers, was surprised to receive a letter from Willa, saying that she planned to come to Red Cloud in November, open the house, and remain through Christmas. Would Lizzie be able to arrange to stay with her and help her?

Lizzie was delighted. It would be like old times!

She opened and cleaned the house, removed dust covers from furniture, had the rooms warm, comfortable, and inviting by the time Willa arrived. And she was pleased to see that coming "home" made Willa glow as in earlier days when she had returned to Red Cloud after a long absence.

Lizzie happily busied herself helping Willa put up Christmas greens, wrap gifts for her old friends, unpack fruit cakes, sherry, and fragrant tea mixes she had brought from New York, and finally—best of all—start the Christmas baking and cooking.

When Willa came plowing through snowdrifts bearing gifts to Annie Pavelka and her family, to Carrie Miner Sherwood and hers, and to the few other girlhood friends remaining in or near Red Cloud, she was received with open arms and hot, hot coffee, and fragrant, fresh *kolaches* and coffee cake. Their "Willie" had come home again!

"It's your own coffee you're gettin'," Annie told her honored guest with a proud smile as, cheeks pink with excitement, she bustled about getting out her best china. Knowing a certain brand of coffee to be Annie's favorite, Willa had long seen to it that she was kept well supplied.

Before the holiday season was over, Willa invited her friends and acquaintances in the village to tea. Among the guests were Mrs. Frank Frisbie and her daughter, Josephine. Mrs. Frisbie had gone to high school with Willa. So had Frank Frisbie, her husband. In fact, Frank had often worked Willa's arithmetic problems for her; mathematics had not been her strong point.

When the guests had all arrived, Willa asked Josephine Frisbie to help her serve. Josephine, working on her Master's Degree at the University of Nebraska, was home for the Christmas holidays. She did not know her hostess as well as her parents did.

The first time she had met Willa had been on the platform of the Burlington Depot in Hastings, Nebraska, where her mother had come to meet her train. Relatives had also come to meet Willa. She was surrounded by a welcoming group when she spied Mrs. Frisbie and broke away to speak to her. Josephine was introduced and they had a brief conversation. "Why, she actually seemed interested in what I was doing!" the girl afterward exclaimed to her mother in some surprise.

Now Josephine liked being asked to help her hostess.

"When we get them served, we'll come back to the kitchen and talk," Willa said to her.

One of the fruitcakes Willa was cutting crumbled considerably and as she was putting the good slices on plates, she said to Josephine, "Scoop up those crumbs and put them in a dish. You and I will eat them later." And to the young woman's amusement, they did!

When the ladies had been served and were busily chatting among themselves, Willa and Josephine sat at the kitchen table and sipped their tea, ate fruitcake crumbs with a spoon, and talked. Most of the time Willa steered the conversation to Josephine's current work on her second degree. Though Josephine had heard it said in Red Cloud that Willa was "cold" and "uppity," she found her quite the opposite, very human though definitely an individualist.

When Willa returned to New York after the holidays, the Menuhins were in town.

The previous spring, when Willa had been in California visiting her mother, Yehudi Menuhin had been on the West Coast, giving concerts. He was then under the management of his father, who was touring with him, so Willa had had further opportunity to get acquainted with the male contingent of the Menuhin family. She had enjoyed getting to know them better. Yehudi responded to Willa with the spontaneous warmth of a child. It seemed perfectly natural to him to have an adult friend. Except for his two small sisters, his was a world of grownups. It was nice that "Aunt Willa" seemed to understand many things without having to be told.

Now all of the Menuhins were in New York in their spacious hotel apartment. Here they happily entertained Willa upon her return to the city. But at the Grosvenor she could not entertain either these new friends or others as she would have liked.

The members of the Cather family had decided to sell the house in Red Cloud, and Willa felt keenly the need of a place she could call home. The time had come when it seemed imperative that she and Edith find an apartment again.

First, though, came another summer at Grand Manan. Willa was much relieved to get away from telephone calls and even personal calls. She was coming to cherish her privacy more and more. This summer the Islanders became particularly aware of her entrenchment.

From Grand Manan, in the early autumn of 1932, Willa and Edith moved, as was their custom, to Jaffrey, New Hampshire—from the summer flowers of the island, to the autumn leaves of New England. And finally from the autumn leaves of New England to the snows of New York, where apartment hunting began in earnest.

In the meantime, Alfred Knopf had in production another book of Willa's. It was not a novel this time, but a collection of three short stories which the author had entitled *Obscure Destinies*. The three were "Neighbor Rossicky," "Old Mrs. Harris," and "Two Friends," all of them quite long for short stories. In all three, Willa had returned to the Nebraska scene, and while some readers thought the old vital flow of emotion had once again flashed forth in them, others thought them "tired," nostalgic and sentimental. Of the three, "Old Mrs. Harris" was generally the most effective. One of these she had written several years before, at the time of her father's death; the other two, after she had completed *Shadows on the Rock*.

Finally, Willa and Edith found an apartment to their liking at 570 Park Avenue. Willa got considerable pleasure from unpacking the old familiar things which had been in storage, and from purchasing such new pieces of furniture as were needed. Yet a weariness had settled upon her which neither the new apartment nor rest seemed to dissipate.

The new apartment consisted of six spacious rooms, so once again Willa could entertain friends. However, the "Friday afternoons" of the old days were not resumed. And even members of her inner circle were received there on increasingly rare occasions. When they did come, they often felt "shut out." At best Willa, with apparent effort, would occasionally break through the protective shell which guarded her more and more, and they would catch a glimpse of the earlier Willa, though minus the vibrant vitality which had always been so much a part of her.

Elizabeth Sergeant's reaction to the Park Avenue apartment, when she called after returning from a prolonged stay in the Southwest, was that it did not go with the Willa Cather she had known. The street, with its "smug," wealthy apartment dwellers, the apartment houses with their liveried doormen and sterile entryways, all spelled "success" and "money" and "self-satisfaction." Weren't these the very things Willa had stood *against?* How could she reconcile herself to living in the midst of them?

The maid brought two glasses of dry sherry. This, at least,

was as it had always been. Elizabeth smiled, thinking how little the cocktail age had touched Willa.

But it seemed strange that Willa had succumbed to the marks of success, and just at the time when the Depression was making miserable the lives of so many.

What Elizabeth did not know was that Willa was helping "her own" through these bad years, giving financial aid not only to some members of her family but also to several farm families on the Divide. She did not know that Willa sent a check for fifty-five dollars to Annie Pavelka to get an electric washer, and then, when she found it had cost sixty-five dollars, insisted on sending the remaining ten, saying, as an excuse, that she wanted Annie to be able to call it "Willie's Washer." Elizabeth knew only that her old friend would not listen to talk of "the New Deal," that she refused to see that any good could come of such government projects as the WPA. So it seemed to her that Willa no longer had sympathy for the needy. The fact was that, as always, Willa found her satisfaction in helping *individuals*.

Elizabeth was to see less and less of her and much of what she saw she did not like. Yet there was a bond between them, and occasionally she saw glimpses of her familiar friend.

Meanwhile Elizabeth mused: True, it was quiet in that apartment. But there was no view. All of the windows looked out on a blank wall.

CHAPTER XXIII

When the Menuhin family arrived in New York that winter, their first thoughts were to get in touch with "Aunt Willa" and things began to happen almost at once.

"Let's send Aunt Willa a great bouquet."

"To let her know we're here."

"And how much we love her."

"And that we want to see her."

"Soon. Very soon."

And then it snowed!

"Oh! Let's see if Aunt Willa will go for a walk in the Park!"

"In the snow."

"She doesn't like the telephone."

"Let's send her a telegram."

"And say, 'Please come for a walk with us in Central Park, in the snow.' "

" 'At your earliest convenience.' "

" 'Signed, Yehudi, Hepzibah, Yaltah.' "

"I get to walk beside her!"

"Me, too!"

"And me!"

"We can't all three walk beside her."

"We'll take turns."

Or:

"Tomorrow's Aunt Willa's birthday."

"What can we do that she'd like most?"

"A basket of fruit?"

"She likes fruit."

"But she likes music best of all."

"The concert! May we take her to the concert with us, Mama?"

They reached out and drew Willa to them, as a family, but even more importantly, as individuals. Yehudi Menuhin, twenty years after her death, still recalled "Aunt Willa" with deep affection. She was vivid and alive in his memory.

"She was invited to dine with us, and to go to concerts with us," he remembered, "but that wasn't the important thing. Those weren't the important times. The important thing for each of the children was getting to talk to her—alone. Then one could use one's private wire, the private wire between oneself and this fine friend.

"We talked about life, and music," Yehudi said, "and the abstractions like integrity—integrity was the soul of the artist; never must one come anywhere near to desecrating or soiling this sacred center of what he was.

"I never remember our talking of politics or world affairs. The longer I knew her, the more I told her my troubles and shared with her my problems, and always she took them seriously and considered them from every side. We talked them over and she helped me to make the decisions which she felt were the right decisions.

"She couldn't stand anything or anyone that wasn't genuine. She was absolutely honest. No one could tempt her with money. Social status or money made no difference to her. It was the people themselves that counted. Every one of us loved her," he said.

"When we took a walk, she would always want to walk around the Reservoir at Ninety-sixth Street in Central Park because, she said, that was the only place in New York where you could walk on earth, not cement."

As a boy he had found this desire of hers to touch earth

delightful; as a man, he still found it delightful—and symbolic of all that she was.

"There was nothing frilly about her," he said, "literally or figuratively. I remember her usually in tailored suits, or a skirt and blouse. She was 'a good sport.' I remember once on my birthday she went coasting with me in Central Park.

"And then she was seriously concerned for us. She thought we didn't have enough exposure to good English literature and the English language, because we were abroad so much. So she asked our mother if we might have a 'Shakespeare Club.' No one was to be admitted but my sisters and me and 'Aunt Willa.' We started reading Shakespeare's plays aloud together. She searched the second-hand bookstores until she found copies of the original Temple editions of the plays for us. Those were wonderful sessions."

Many years later Yehudi Menuhin discovered a complete Temple edition in a secondhand store in New Orleans and purchased it with joy. Nor did he forget to write "Aunt Willa" to tell her about it.

What was it that drew Willa Cather so strongly to this highly talented and cultured Jewish family? Were they, to her, a reincarnation of the Weiners of Red Cloud? Had she now at long last attained an equal footing with the type of people whom she had always most admired?

Whatever her reasons, it was a delightful, creative, rewarding friendship on both sides: for each of the Menuhin children, for their mother Marutha Menuhin, and, though to a lesser degree, for Moshe Menuhin, their father—and for Willa.

Even though to most of her friends she seemed to be tiring and growing old at this time, to Yehudi Menuhin, in retrospect, "Aunt Willa" seemed to have been young in heart.

But her public image now was austere and far from warm. When the French, whom Willa had so long admired, in turn showed their respect for her by awarding her the *Prix Femina Américaine* for *Shadows on the Rock,* she demurred at the idea of accepting it publicly. However, the committee in charge, though somewhat annoyed at what they considered a show of temperament, got her to appear by promising they would allow no photographers at the affair. The men of the press, however, had a job to do and they did it. When Willa stood to receive the prize, flashbulbs popped like Fourth of July fireworks. What the cameras registered was the celebrated novelist with a look of horror frozen on her face.

CHAPTER XXIV

Willa had begun another novel in the spring of 1933, shortly after the publication of *Obscure Destinies*. But her intimate friends noted that her progress on it was slow and fitful. It proved to be her last book but one. At sixty, she was beginning to feel the weight of her years, and her writing showed it. By her own admission, she was very tired. Old friends said that when they saw Willa now, she appeared somehow smaller, her face thinner, and the old hearty smile was gone.

During that summer, at Grand Manan, Edith Lewis observed that Willa worked on the new novel only fitfully.

Yet in the fall, back at the Shattuck Inn in Jaffrey, the Austermanns saw very much the same Willa Cather they had always seen. They noted her happiness in the view of Mt. Monadnock, in the turning foliage, in the bright but sharp autumn days as the season progressed. They saw her following the same routine as in former years. They felt that she was happy in her writing.

The writing did go well at Jaffrey and the first draft of the novel, *Lucy Gayheart*, was completed there.

But all this was to be short-lived.

Back in New York, when she began making revisions on the manuscript and typing it from her handwritten copy as was her habit, her right wrist began to pain her. It became swollen and inflamed, and she was forced to consult a doctor.

The orthopedic surgeon to whom she was finally referred diagnosed it as a severely inflamed tendon sheath. The hand required complete immobilization.

It was spring before she could go back to work on the manuscript. In the meantime, friends became aware of her fierce independence. Despite the difficulty of doing for herself, she preferred not to be helped. Often for weeks and even months at a time, her hand and wrist were encased in a heavy metal and leather brace which, in effect, made her one-handed. Yet she struggled determinedly to dress herself, to do her own hair.

She was able to finish preparing *Lucy Gayheart* for the publisher during that summer of 1934 at Grand Manan, but the difficulty with her wrist—sometimes with both wrists—was to return again and again during her remaining years, and to make any sustained effort at writing and performing other tasks increasingly difficult.

Except during the winter season at the concert halls in New York, Willa was now seldom seen in public. Neither opera house nor theater saw her as of old.

A change occurred, too, in her musical preferences. While in earlier years her greatest passion had been opera, now it was the concert of the individual artist. Perhaps this was due in part to the influence of the Menuhins.

Besides the Menuhins, Willa made another new friend among the younger generation during her later years. He was an English poet, Stephen Tennant. Their friendship began while he was still at the Slade School in London and read *Lost Lady*. He wrote her, expressing his delight with the novel. Willa replied, and a correspondence ensued which lasted ten years before Stephen Tennant came to the United States and the two met.

Young Tennant thought her "most beautiful to look at, with dark blue eyes and auburn hair . . . . She was very elegant" and, he said, "such fun! We used to walk in Central Park in rain and snow, Willa's eyes full of laughter, her cheeks pink."

He found to his delight that she was an admirer of Thomas Hardy's novels. When he told her he had met Hardy and that Hardy had spoken appreciatively of her work, the friendship was solidified. To some of her old friends whom Willa Cather now often "shut out," it must have seemed strange that she found energy to expend on her newer and younger friends. But perhaps, reluctant to join the ranks of the aging, she gained reassurance from the young.

At any rate, Stephen Tennant, in looking back on the years of his friendship with Willa, remembered her as "very simple and very complex." He found her "very proud, a subtle woman, shy, reticent, very intellectual indeed, a mystic." He said of her—even though these were "the dimming years"—that she was "sometimes beautiful, always vivid. . . .

"She was like the American earth," he said, "rich, unpredictable, fecund. Somber, in a way. Loyal, wise, deeply loving and tender."

But he could smile at her human foibles. One of her loves, he remembered, was making ice cream. He recalled Rebecca West's account of visiting her. Just when Rebecca would be enjoying a *bon mot*, he said, Willa would vanish into the kitchen, to be gone for as much as half an hour at a time. Then ice cream would be forthcoming!

But her new friends were not of the avant garde. They were people to whom Willa could talk about art and letters without having the "unworthy" ideas of the "new generation" thrust upon her. Such friends did not upset her because they held to the kind of ideals which meant everything to her.

The year 1935 was probably the first year since she was sixteen that Willa Cather did no writing, though that year saw the publication of *Lucy Gayheart*.

For that Willa had chosen an apt name for her principal character. It was Dickinsonian, for Lucy Gayheart was exactly what her name implied; she was attractive, well liked by all, talented as a pianist, vivacious, and given to wholesome good times—particularly ice skating. Harry Gordon, the catch of Haverford, Nebraska, squired her when he had the time and inclination from his multiple inheritance and business affairs. In contrast to Lucy's disposition was that of her older sister; practical and uncreative, Pauline had been Lucy's "mother" since that parent's death. Their father, Jacob, a watchmaker by trade and a violinist by nature, had denied himself and Pauline so that Lucy might study in Chicago.

Lucy's bright disposition remained until the accidental drowning in Europe of Clement Sebastian to whom she had been practice accompanist. Her freshness, charm, and earnestness had attracted him. And though he was married, his suavity, gentleness, and exceptional voice had caused Lucy to fall in love with him. Their professional plans, which were to take effect after his return to Chicago, had been high.

But the sudden tragedy threw Lucy into despair, and she returned to Haverford where she remained lethargic and disinterested in people and matters.

While Lucy and Sebastian had been working in Chicago, Harry Gordon had visited her and had bluntly proposed. Lucy had replied by blurting a lie, that she "had gone all the way" with her local love. On the rebound, Harry quickly married Harriet Arkwright, a plain but shrewd and wealthy woman from St. Joseph, Missouri.

After quite some time in her Haverford hiatus, Lucy with her sister and father attended *The Bohemian Girl,* performed by a traveling opera troupe. Though the production was far from excellent, it served to inspire Lucy to return to Chicago. She quietly, secretly made plans.

Unknowing of these, even when they were far advanced, Pauline brightly reported to Lucy that she had found two piano pupils for her. Characteristically, Lucy burst forth about her determination to return to cultural Chicago and then rushed from the house to go skating on the river. She had not been told about the river's change of channel; she fell through the ice and was drowned. The same manner of death for Lucy and for her lover seems to the reader more coincidental than deliberate; the townspeople thought it was the latter.

Book Three, though only about one-tenth of the novel, was concerned with Harry Gordon's introspection twenty-five years later, some time after Pauline's death and shortly after the death of Jacob.

Though Willa Cather had said that she was fascinated by singers and by actors (numbering the Otis Skinners and the George Arlisses among her friends), she was here preoccupied, as in *The Song of the Lark,* by a heroine with musical talent rather than one who was a stage personality. And again, in *Lucy Gayheart,* there were touches of sentiment. As with a number of Willa's other stories, she showed the loneliness of the sensitive and gifted in a sparsely cultural, sparsely intellectual community, and she portrayed their groping for far, wider horizons.

Inevitably, comparisons were made between *Lucy Gayheart* and *The Song of the Lark,* though the themes of the books differed; and, also inevitably, *Lucy Gayheart* suffered.

Some critics were more caustic than others, but the general consensus was that Willa Cather had lost her swift and delicate sureness of touch, that the book had a heaviness, the plot was contrived, and even that the novel lacked substance. Her powers of characterization, however, remained intact and Lucy's was a rounded and skillful portraiture.

CHAPTER XXV

In the spring of 1935, the Hambourgs returned to the United States, for Isabelle was desperately ill with the affliction that had been growing progressively worse for years. In fact, when the Hambourgs first arrived in New York, Isabelle was hospitalized, and Willa visited her daily. Later, when the invalid had improved somewhat and her husband had to go to Chicago for a concert, she wished to accompany him, so Willa went with them to help make things easier for her. For the five months the Hambourgs remained in the States, Willa devoted most of her time to them.

The following winter and spring, although she did little new writing, Willa edited and reworked several of her critical essays that had appeared from time to time in various publications. These were for a small volume which she entitled *Not Under Forty*. She worked through the summer of 1936 on this project, writing one new essay and a very brief prefatory note.

This note was of special interest because it once again underscored her oft-quoted statement, "The world broke in two in 1922 or thereabouts," and reflected her consistent disillusionment with the state of things after the First World War. She had seen great promise in the first-generation pioneers; she saw it running out in the second. She had held high hopes that the idealism of the founders of our nation would be maintained; she saw their idealism being smothered by materialism. She was out of step as the twentieth century went bumbling on its way.

Yet when Yehudi Menuhin was asked whether he remembered her as disillusioned with the times (in the 1930's when he saw most of her), his reply was in the negative.

Not Under Forty was published before the year was out, and in late fall Willa began writing a long short story, "The Old Beauty," which she was able to complete by early spring.

Another editorial project was engaging her attention at this time, the publication of a definitive "subscription" edition of her complete works by Houghton Mifflin. First came the business negotiations in regard to this edition.

Although Willa seemed to hold the pursuit of the dollar in American society in disdain, she drove a good bargain in her own financial negotiations. As Elizabeth Sergeant had noted in regard to the choice of the Park Avenue apartment, when it came close to home, Willa seemed to enjoy affluence.

Having at length signed an agreement with Houghton Mifflin, Willa began editing her published works. She did considerable cutting, particularly in *Song of the Lark* and in the introduction to *My Antonia*.

But this work was not creative. For three years now she had written little, and then, short pieces only. Edith Lewis noticed how sorely Willa missed the sustaining endeavor involved in writing a novel. Working on a long piece of fiction had always given unity and purpose to her life. It was with relief that Edith saw her begin *Sapphira and the Slave Girl* in the fall of 1937. It was to be her last novel.

The new work was to be a story of the Virginia of her early childhood and, in the spring of 1938, Willa suggested that she and Edith make a trip to Winchester. This they did, and it proved to be a successful rendezvous with the past.

In Virginia as at Jaffrey, at Grand Manan, in Southern France, in the Southwest, and in Nebraska, Willa responded warmly to the beauties of nature. It was the season in which the acacia trees and the dogwood were in bloom, and the wild azaleas ran rampant with their riot of pink and red blossoms. Willa gathered these wild flowers by the armload and seemed literally to revel in their freshness and beauty.

Although she did not ask permission to go into the big brick house which had been her earliest remembered home, she stood and gazed down upon it from the highway which had been built above it. And although she commented on the run-down, desolate appearance of her old home, she did not seem to be depressed by it. Edith thought it was as if she were looking at the house as it actually was, but seeing it as it had been in 1880.

It was three years before the novel of Old Virginia was ready for the publisher. They were three extremely difficult years for Willa.

First, the death of Isabelle McClung Hambourg occurred in Sorrento, Italy, in 1938. After her death, Jan returned to Willa all of the letters she had written Isabelle over the years. Each weekend, until they were all gone, Willa had Edith take a large bundle of them to the apartment-house incinerator to be burned. She had not looked inside them. She was destroying a lifetime's communication with a beloved friend; surely she was burning a part of herself. Nor would she look at the flame or the ashes.

Although difficult to understand, this act was consistent with a clause in her will which was later to deny publication of or quotation from any of her personal letters.

Second, another death occurred during the writing of *Sapphira*, that of Willa's brother Douglass. It had come suddenly and, as with Isabelle's death, brought Willa a sense of irreconcilable loss.

Finally, the refuge to which she had returned for many years, the writing sanctuary at Jaffrey, New Hampshire, was literally ripped up by the roots. A severe hurricane struck Jaffrey in the summer of 1938, destroying great stretches of beautiful pines and hurling them by the giant handful into grotesque heaps, leaving swaths of pitted emptiness where once had been green-walled, sun-mottled cathedrals. Among the lovely lost spots was Willa's outdoor studio.

She did not visit Jaffrey after the 1938 hurricane, although nine years later her body would be laid to its permanent rest in the peaceful little cemetery upon which Mt. Monadnock looked down as it had upon the little garret room at the Shattuck Inn.

Sapphira and the Slave Girl appeared in 1940. It was a stronger novel than *Lucy Gayheart,* but still it was not among Willa's best.

The character of Sapphira dominated the book, and the author's characterization of this Southern woman was astute.

Sapphira, at the time of coming into her inheritance, had married a miller and, with him, had come from a more wealthy and cultured part of the state to the Back Creek area of Virginia. With her, she had brought her slaves.

At the opening of the story, the couple were well into middle age and had a widowed daughter, Rachel Blake, and two granddaughters living nearby. Sapphira, a proud and handsome woman, had become a semi-invalid.

Without any real basis, Sapphira became jealous of one of her slave girls, Nancy, who took care of the miller's quarters in the Mill House. So she invited a nephew, renowned for his affairs with women, to pay the family an extended visit. Once he had arrived, she did all she could to throw Nancy into his clutches. Nancy, frightened, fled to the home of Sapphira's daughter Rachel for protection. Eventually, Rachel helped her to escape to Canada via the Underground Railroad. This brought a rupture in the family, which was not repaired until one of the granddaughters died of diphtheria. Then Rachel and her one remaining child were invited to come live with Sapphira and the miller.

The last section of the novel took place twenty-five years later, and was called "Nancy's Return." Sapphira and her husband had died. But Rachel Blake and Nancy's mother,

Till, still lived at Back Creek. It was to them that the freed-woman Nancy returned for a visit. She had long been housekeeper for a wealthy family in Montreal, had married, and had a fine family of her own. The three, reunited, talked over old times, with Sapphira at the center of their reminiscences. For Sapphira, while not always lovable or admirable, was a strong character.

This codicil-type ending Willa used in several of her novels. It was as if she wished to handle all possible contingencies herself, leaving as little to the imagination of the reader as the do-everything dolls leave to the imagination of a child.

In this last novel, Willa had turned to "the irrevocable past," and some critics felt it was an elegiac and pathetic past that seemed very far away.

Willa herself was receding further and further into this "irrevocable past." From it also, she had drawn the material for the story, "The Old Beauty," which was not published until 1948, after her death, when, with two other stories, Knopf brought out *The Old Beauty and Others*.

Also published posthumously by Knopf was a little volume entitled *Willa Cather on Writing*. It contained four prefaces, four letters, four essays, and one "fragment." This compilation summarized well the author's beliefs about writing. The volume brought the total of her published works to nineteen.

CHAPTER XXVI

In the long view, covering Willa Cather's total literary output, two characteristics of her work which were also dominant personal traits stand out: strength and sensitivity. Paradoxically, the strength of the novels may be elusive, but their sensitivity can be more readily understood.

Stephen Tennant in his essay, "The Room Beyond," which Alfred Knopf used to preface *Willa Cather on Writing*, attempted to analyze it: "As a novelist," he wrote, "Willa Cather has a naturalness so great that one is tempted to think of her almost as not a writer at all . . . this rare and attaching naturalness has its birth in her deepest being. . . . It is the stamp of her unchallengeable integrity and it animates her serene and often unstressed prose with a *pure current of power*." Surely the strength of her art is compounded of many elements.

It is in characterization and sensory image that sensitivity in her writing is most evident. René Rapin, writing critically of Willa Cather's works, called her characters "the high-water mark of her art . . . her most precious legacy to the world." Another critic, Mr. T. K. Whipple, said her imagery gave "full-bodied solidity as well as beauty to her work."

Strength and sensitivity have been remarked in all her novels.

Even though some critics accused Willa Cather of neglecting the world of the twentieth century for the past, she may have been wise to choose to write upon only those subjects which "teased her mind," as Sarah Orne Jewett had admonished her to do. It was in this material that she was most at home.

Her material was essentially that of biography and portraiture, each novel the life story of one character, in most cases based upon that of someone who had actually lived; the characters in her stories were usually pioneers or artists, and they were heroic individuals. Elizabeth Sergeant said Willa's passion for artists, especially musicians, was second only to her passion for pioneers.

Landscape also was an important part of her material: the Nebraska prairies, the Southwest desert, the "Rock" of Quebec, and finally, the Virginia of her very young years. Her use of it was effective as symbol, and integral in her production of mood and atmosphere. "Few novels are so full of the sights and sounds and smells of the earth as Miss Cather's," wrote N. Elizabeth Monroe in *The Novel and Society*. Miss Cather's sense impressions were always vivid and added much to the total effect of place and portrait.

To these materials of pioneer peoples and places and artists in alien environments, Willa took her own attitudes and patterns of thought; and through the combination she delineated her themes.

One might say "theme" rather than "themes," as basically her central concern was always "the passionate struggle of a tenacious will," taking the form of a conflict between the superior individual and an unworthy society. The basic Cather theme has been described as "conquest," as "corruption," or as "quest." The first-generation pioneers, she seemed to be saying, were endowed with creative power and imagination, but their sons and daughters—except for a few artists—had degenerated and succumbed to the materialistic society, valuing only ease, and money, and *things*. Much has been said about the sub-theme in her later novels—strong antipathy for the machine age.

In her characterizations, Willa Cather did an artful job: Her characters became vital, real people; they were three-dimensional, individualized, drawn surely but economically.

Walter Fuller Taylor in *Story of American Letters* said that there were few writers who have produced a greater number of "genuinely human, clearly revealed, distinctly individualized characters." He said she "attained a deft economy of characterization hardly equaled in the modern novel." Her method of characterization, in general, is a presentation of her characters "from the inside."

There has been some criticism of the men in her stories, who many readers have felt were never truly masculine, and of her "unrealistic" portrayal of some other people whom she did not involve in dramatic relations with each other. It has been suggested that her women are always in mother or daughter relationship to men, never truly lovers. Her characters have been said by some to be all of a piece in emotional involvement—an inelastic piece which does not stretch to encompass nearly all of human nature. One observer has written that all of her characters smell of Ivory soap—even "the bad women."

But on one phase of Willa's art—her style—critics have agreed whole-heartedly. Intangible as style is, there is ample evidence to prove that hers can be termed fine, artistic, beautiful, and even classical. It is economical, controlled, and disciplined, refined and fastidious, clear and sharp. Its economy may be credited to her exact word choice, apt use of simile and metaphor, and symbolism. Her style is never an end in itself, but always a fitting implement.

Some have seen symbolism in her characters; some in her setting. All have made note of her symbolic use of the rock. Professor Brown called this her "ultimate" symbol, and characterized her rock as "stratified" and "immovable."

Sometimes Willa Cather's stories have been criticized for having little or no plot. But Professor E. K. Brown has said that she had "no capacity or desire" to construct intricate, tightly structured plots. Harry Hartwick, an American Literature specialist, said that more and more she came to base her stories on the biographies of her characters, "and to lean toward the *naturalistic* method in their tendency to follow the lines of human growth."

Whether this "lack of plot," or "naturalistic approach," is a strength or a weakness, depends on the point of view. Today, "plot" in the restricted sense of the word is considered by many an artifice, so that looseness of plot is scarcely a fault.

In addition to being classified by some as in the school of naturalism, Willa Cather's work has been associated by others with the school of humanism. She portrayed the interdependence of Man in struggle, in suffering, in love, and in friendship.

The superior qualities of her work are her sensitivity, her originality, her pure—almost classical—style, her restraint, her careful elimination of extraneous material, her portrayal of character, and her integrity. Against the American literary scene of the twentieth century Willa Cather looms large—as her plowshare stood large against the prairie horizon.

CHAPTER XXVII

The tragedy of Pearl Harbor took place on Willa's sixty-eighth birthday. With the Second World War, with her increasing illness, and with the loss of another beloved brother, Roscoe, she isolated herself even from her dearest friends.

The following summer it was necessary for her to have a gall-bladder operation and to remain in the city during the hot months. Nor was she at any time thereafter able to return to Grand Manan. Travel during the war years was too difficult.

Yet on occasion the curtain lifted and one or another of her friends would smile with pleasure, having caught a glimpse of the warm and generous Willa they had known over the years; a glimpse of the vibrant, responsive, sensitive person they had cherished.

To the oldest friends in Red Cloud, particularly to Carrie Miner Sherwood, warmth and generosity still shone out in the letters received from Willa. In some there were enclosed sizable checks for the Webster County Red Cross from "an unidentified source." Or Willa wrote Carrie how good she thought it was of her to spend such long hours and so much energy in Red Cross work, and closed with an admonition not "to overdo." Carrie appreciated *being appreciated* by her old and very dear friend.

There had been a flash of the old Willa when she wrote scornfully of successful businessmen and attorneys who seemed to find it necessary to make their handwriting as illegible as possible. Willa's own writing was almost indecipherable at times, reminding Carrie of a series of irregularly jutting foothills.

And even though Willa had been ill, Carrie wasn't surprised to learn from her letters that she was doing much of the housework and all of the grocery shopping, which the war made so difficult. Carrie thought it generous of Willa, with her bad wrist and lack of help in the apartment, to keep the letters coming.

To newer friends of the past decade or so, Willa was still responsive when they visited her on occasion on Park Avenue.

All three of the Menuhin young people had married, and with their families, they had scattered. Hepzibah was living in Australia. Yehudi was giving benefit concerts abroad and at home for War Relief, but when he was in New York, he always went to see "Aunt Willa."

And so there was a last time. It was March of 1947, and Hepzibah, her husband and their two little boys were on a visit "home." She and Yehudi had been in concert at the Metropolitan and "Aunt Willa" had gone to hear them. They saw that she was very frail, but still they saw the face of their beloved friend, of their "almost Father-Confessor." Yehudi was leaving for England; Hepzibah also was leaving New York. Together they planned to go to "Aunt Willa's" apartment to take their children to see her, if she were strong enough. Hepzibah called on the morning of the day they were to depart. Yes, of course "Aunt Willa" would see them; she would be delighted to meet Hepzibah's little boys.

Shortly after Hepzibah and her family arrived at the apartment on Park Avenue, her brother arrived with his little son and daughter. And though their children were seeing a more fragile and faded Willa Cather than their parents had known in their childhood, Yehudi and Hepzibah were grateful that their children might know "Aunt Willa" even briefly.

On April 24, only about a month later, Willa Cather died in the apartment in which she had lived for fifteen years, in the presence of the friend with whom she had been for forty years.

There was a public service in New York, but the final,

quiet one at Jaffrey Center, on the slope below the large white church, known as "the Old Meeting House," was the appropriate one.

In an article in the *Monadnock Ledger* of May 9, a resident of Jaffrey wrote: "It is almost as if the title of her first book of verse, *April Twilights,* was a portent of things to come, for it was late afternoon on a dark April day when her body arrived in Jaffrey for burial services in the Old Burying Yard.

"Jaffrey feels a deep sense of pride in that Willa Cather chose to come here on her fall vacations to seek seclusion and rest, and a solemn sense of honor that in death she came here for final rest in a secluded spot in the Old Burying Yard, overlooking the mountain that she loved."

The simple white stone at her grave bears the inscription:

THE TRUTH AND CHARITY OF HER GREAT SPIRIT

WILL LIVE ON IN THE WORK

WHICH IS HER ENDURING GIFT

TO HER COUNTRY AND ALL ITS PEOPLE

Beneath it is a quotation from *My Antonia*: ". . . that is happiness; to be dissolved into something complete and great."

The day was cold and wet when her body arrived at Jaffrey. The simple but heavy casket of bronze required eight bearers. They came from the New York mortuary, impersonal and somber in black cutaways and striped trousers. There was only a handful of mourners, including Willa's two remaining brothers, John and James, from California, a niece and nephew, and Edith Lewis. In the gathering dark, a little boy sat on the cemetery wall, dangling his legs, quiet, watching, listening. The casket, which had remained unopened, was lowered into the earth. The only music was the thud of clods against it. There were no flowers.

Suggestions for Further Reading

Books by Willa Cather

The Troll Garden. (New York: McClure, Phillips & Co., 1905) (Also Signet paperback, New American Library)

PUBLISHED BY HOUGHTON MIFFLIN CO., BOSTON:

Alexander's Bridge, 1912
O Pioneers!, 1913. (Also Sentry paperback, Houghton Mifflin)
The Song of the Lark, 1915. (Also Sentry paperback, Houghton Mifflin)
My Antonia, 1918. (Also Sentry paperback, Houghton Mifflin)

PUBLISHED BY ALFRED A. KNOPF, INC., NEW YORK:

Youth and the Bright Medusa, 1920
One of Ours, 1922
April Twilights and Other Poems, 1923
A Lost Lady, 1923
The Professor's House, 1925
My Mortal Enemy, 1926. (Also Vintage paperback, Random House)
Death Comes for the Archbishop, 1927
Shadows on the Rock, 1931
Obscure Destinies, 1932
Lucy Gayheart, 1935
Not Under Forty, 1936
Sapphira and the Slave Girl, 1940
The Old Beauty and Others, 1948
Willa Cather on Writing, 1949
Willa Cather in Europe, 1956. Ed. by Kates, George N.

OTHERS:

April Twilights. Ed. by Slote, Bernice. (Lincoln: U. of Nebr. Press, rev. ed., 1968) (Also Bison paperback, U. of Nebr. Press)
Early Stories of Willa Cather. Ed. by Bennett, Mildred R. (New York: Dodd, Mead, 1957) (Also Apollo paperback)
Five Stories. (New York: Random House, 1956. Vintage paperback)
The Kingdom of Art. Ed. by Slote, Bernice. (Lincoln: U. of Nebr. Press, 1966)

Willa Cather's Collected Short Fiction, 1892–1912. Ed. by Bennett, Mildred R. (Lincoln: U. of Nebr. Press, text ed., 1965)

Writings from Willa Cather's Campus Years. Ed. by Shiveley, James R. (Lincoln: U. of Nebr. Press, 1950)

Jewett, Sarah Orne, *The Country of the Pointed Firs and Other Stories.* Selected and arranged with a preface by Willa Cather. (Garden City, N. Y.: Doubleday, 1927)

Books about Willa Cather

Bennett, Mildred R., *The World of Willa Cather.* (New York: Dodd, Mead, 1951) (Also Bison paperback, U. of Nebr. Press, rev. ed., 1961)

Bloom, Edward A. and Lillian D., *Willa Cather's Gift of Sympathy.* (Carbondale: Southern Ill. U. Press, 1962) (Hardcover and paperback)

Brown, Edward K. (completed by Leon Edel), *Willa Cather.* (New York: Alfred A. Knopf, 1953)

Daiches, David, *Willa Cather, A Critical Introduction.* (Ithaca, N. Y.: Cornell U. Press, 1951)

Giannone, Richard, *Music in Willa Cather's Fiction.* (Lincoln: U. of Nebr. Press, 1968)

Lewis, Edith, *Willa Cather, Living.* (New York: Alfred A. Knopf, 1953)

Randall, John H., III, *The Landscape and the Looking Glass.* (Boston: Houghton Mifflin, 1960)

Rapin, Rene, *Willa Cather.* (New York: Robert M. McBride, 1930)

Sergeant, Elizabeth Shepley, *Willa Cather, A Memoir.* (Philadelphia and New York, Lippincott, 1953) (Also Bison paperback, U. of Nebr. Press, 1963)

INDEX